# Reviews of Chamberlain Law Group Ltd.

*Richard Chamberlain was highly recommended to us by a friend attorney who felt he could meet our needs. He was most helpful when sorting out everything for us with the death of our mother. Since working closely with him for her will, we decided to proceed with Richard in having a trust done for us. He was not only helpful and understanding of our needs, he gives you the understanding and confidence that is needed when working on something that is very important to us. Can not recommend him enough to anyone who has questions and concerns to make the experience easy.*

\- Claudette Bretzloff

*My husband and I were referred to Richard Chamberlain by our financial advisor. We were thoroughly impressed with Richard and his assistant Char when it came to updating our Will. We were educated on the different Estate Planning options (which can be overwhelming). Richard simplified it with diagrams and written material, making sure we completely understood and chose the best option for our family. I fully trust that if something were to happen to my husband and I, Richard will work with our family in assuring the best for our children. We highly recommend Chamberlain Law Group!*

\- Julie Calkins Barfield

*My wife and I worked with Richard to redo our trusts, wills and other related legal documents. Richard took what could have been a complicated discussion and simplified it so we could understand each of the steps along the way. We highly recommend the Chamberlain Law Group for your legal needs!*

\- Venzel Communications

*Richard is a great communicator and listener. He explains complex subjects in a clear way. He also uses diagrams well to illustrate concepts. The Trust and Will he created for my wife and I are very well organized. This is the third iteration of a Will for my wife and I (priors were other practices) and by far the most satisfying experience.*

zjdalton

I0030084

*Our experience in setting up our Estate was Awesome!! Richard is so very knowledgeable in the many many scenarios that make up the planning of your estate. I would highly recommend Richard to anyone who needs this service. He took as much or as little time as we required to get everything set up just the way that we wanted.*

-Brian Brandenburg

*I met with Richard Chamberlain to inquire about estate planning. Prior to our meeting he sent me a packet of information that outlined in clear, understandable terms information I needed to think about. At our appointment he guided me through the estate planning process and was responsive to questions I asked. His professional, reassuring and knowledgeable demeanor was very comforting. He made clear what could have been a very confusing process. I would highly recommend his firm to anyone in need of this type of service.*

- Sandra Tosha

*Richard was very thorough in preparing our estate plan. He answered all of our questions, offered guidance as to what would be best for our goals, and explained everything during the final meeting to sign the paperwork. I highly recommend using Chamberlain Law Group for your estate planning needs.*

- Barb Wilson

*Richard Chamberlain of Chamberlain Law handled my Estate Planning. What a relief to have this done! Not only did Richard explain things in a way I could easily understand but he also made sure my plan was complete. I would highly recommend him and his law firm!*

- Jennifer Glacken

# PROTECTING YOUR
# FAMILY'S FUTURE

## ALL ABOUT WILLS, TRUSTS & PROBATE

RICHARD M. CHAMBERLAIN, ESQ.

WORD ASSOCIATION PUBLISHERS
www.wordassociation.com
1.800.827.7903

ISBN: 978-1-63385-392-8

*Designed and published by*
Word Association Publishers
205 Fifth Avenue
Tarentum, Pennsylvania 15084

www.wordassociation.com
1.800.827.7903

# Table of Contents

# Introduction

This book is about making plans to protect yourself and your loved ones and to preserve your assets. It's about how to make an estate plan that will accomplish your needs and goals. It's about identifying pitfalls and opportunities in your estate plan, and making the most of the process.

I wrote this book for two reasons. First, I wrote this book to help take some of the mystery and complexity out of estate planning for you. In order to make the best estate plan possible, I believe that people must have a solid foundation of understanding of the issues involved in making an effective estate plan. In my law firm, we spend a lot of time teaching our clients the things they need to know to make their plan meet their planning needs. In our educational seminars and in our consultations with our clients, we teach the fundamental issues involved so that they can understand and determine not only what type of plan to use, but also why it's the best plan for them. This book is designed to help you do the same things.

In working with my clients, I want them to be well-informed about why the planning they end up doing is the most appropriate for them, after looking at all of the various planning options available for them. You may see this approach as different from any other attorneys you've worked with. And that's really my goal – to be different from other attorneys.

We're here to serve our clients by helping them through difficult issues and difficult times, by teaching them how to understand the issues surrounding estate planning, by making the complex more understandable, and by preparing the legal documents that will meet their needs and goals.

The second reason I wrote this book is because a lot of people are hearing a lot of misinformation and bad "legal advice" from other advisors, both lawyers and non-lawyers alike. For example, a lot of attorneys who don't do estate planning every day will tell their clients that there's no reason to do a living trust and that a Will is all that is needed. In a lot of those situations a trust would have been very beneficial and would have saved the client's family thousands or even tens of thousands of dollars. I hear financial advisors telling their clients that the only reason to do a trust is if they have millions of dollars. As we'll see later in the book, trusts are about so much more than saving estate taxes and can be used to accomplish so many planning goals. We see bank employees advising their customers just to put beneficiary designations on their accounts, and even though that approach might work to accomplish one planning goal, it may fail to accomplish the customer's other goals. We'll explore all of these issues throughout this book.

When I graduated from law school back in 1992, I will admit that I knew almost nothing about estate planning and had no interest in learning about it. I was going to be a litigator, arguing cases on behalf of my clients in front of juries and helping bring the truth to light. It didn't take me long, however, to discover that I don't have the personality for litigation. I am not a confrontational person, and while I enjoyed the strategy of litigation, I didn't enjoy anything else about it.

About three years later, a good friend of mine introduced me to estate planning. He was a financial advisor and had a client who needed to do estate planning. I explained to Rusty that I really didn't know much about it, but with his encouragement I started to learn. And while I was learning about the legal-technical aspects of estate planning, I also learned that I love this kind of work.

Estate planning, for me, is an opportunity to be a teacher and counselor for my clients. It's an opportunity to connect with people, to learn about them and their families, to teach them about some difficult topics, and to help them discover how to help themselves and their loved ones. Together we can make plans that will anticipate potential problems that can arise in the future and take steps to avoid those problems before they happen. So instead of being the advocate in the courtroom after problems come to the surface, I can be the guide who helps my clients avoid the problems in the first place.

Admittedly estate planning isn't at the top of most people's list of favorite topics. As an estate planning attorney, I meet and talk with people every day who would rather be almost anywhere else, talking about almost anything else. Let's face it: talking about the possibility of our own incapacity and about our own deaths isn't the most uplifting of topics. To make matters worse, it can be complicated, with lots of choices surrounding lots of issues. But as uncomfortable and as complex as it can be, we also understand that making plans and facing the possibilities is the loving, responsible and right thing to do.

This book is written for anyone who has assets and who has loved ones and/or causes that they want to provide for. It's not written specifically for any age group or for people who have assets above a certain amount. If you have assets and people and/or causes you care about, then the information in this book will be helpful to you as you evaluate your current estate planning and think about the changes you need to make.

If you're expecting a dry, boring, technical dissertation of estate planning law, then I hope you'll be pleasantly surprised by this book. I've written this book more like the conversations I have with clients in my conference room or with people who attend one of our estate planning seminars, using plain English and examples that help illustrate the concepts. My goal was to write something that you can pick up and read and understand.

The information will be understandably generic, but in order to make the best estate plan for you, I recommend that you meet with an experienced estate planning attorney to apply the principles you learn in this book to your particular situation. After doing so, your estate plan will be customized for you, and will meet your particular planning needs in the best possible way.

I hope the information presented in this book is helpful to you. If you would like more information about any of the topics raised here, you can call our office at 419-872-7670, or you can visit our website at www.chamberlain-law.net.

*The contents of this book are for informational purposes only and should not be construed as legal advice for any particular situation. If you require legal advice and/or want to engage in any estate planning, you should consult with an experienced estate planning attorney.*

# Section 1

# *Estate Planning 101*

B efore I get into the specifics about the issues affecting your estate planning decisions, I want to first give you the background you need to make sense of these issues. In this first section of the book we'll cover some preliminary estate planning concepts and then look at the different kinds of estate plans available to you.

This probably won't come as a news flash to you: there is no "one size fits all" type of estate plan. There's not any one kind of planning that's right for everyone. There's an old saying that if the only tool you have in your toolbox is a hammer, then every problem will look like a nail. In order to make your best estate plan be the one that is most appropriate for you and be the one that will meet your planning needs and goals, you need to take a look at all of the planning tools in the toolbox. If your problem is a nail, then the hammer can be used. If, instead, your problem requires an Allen wrench, then that should be used instead. The type of planning that is appropriate for you will depend on your personal situation, your financial situation, your beneficiaries, and your planning goals.

As we go through this first section of the book, we'll examine each of the planning solutions and strategies to see how they work (or don't work) to achieve planning goals.

# Chapter 1

# *What is Estate Planning?*

B efore we start looking into the issues surrounding estate planning, it's important to get some preliminary issues out of the way first. If you've never done any estate planning (or even if you *have* done some planning, but you didn't do your planning with an experienced estate planning attorney), you may not know even what estate planning is all about.

## What is Estate Planning?

In order to understand what estate planning is, it's helpful to know what estate planning isn't. First, estate planning isn't a tool reserved for the rich. Estate planning isn't limited to estate tax reduction planning only for high net worth families.

I'll sometimes have people come into my office for an initial consultation, and they'll ask if they have "enough assets" to make estate planning necessary. That's really not the right question. I tell them that you do not need to be "wealthy" to need estate planning. You simply need to have property you want to control during your lifetime, and then ultimately distribute to your loved ones upon your passing in the most effective and efficient manner possible.

Simply put, "estate planning" is a *"process of planning for a person's assets to be used during their lifetime consistent with their needs and goals and then distributed to a person's loved ones, also in way that meets their needs and goals."* It's a process that allows and enables you to make a plan for (1) how your estate will be managed in the event of your incapacity, (2) how to pass your estate to your loved ones - when you want and the way you want, and (3) how to be as efficient as possible - minimizing expenses and taxes, passing as much as possible of what you have accumulated in your lifetime to your loved ones.

Sometimes people are surprised to hear that estate planning involves how their property will be handled before they pass away. These people see estate planning solely as putting together a legal document to distribute their assets upon their death. In my experience, having a plan for a possible incapacity is just as important as the plan for the disposition of assets after death.

Notice that in the definition above, I stated that estate planning was a "process." Many people believe that estate planning is something that is done once, and that it can then be forgotten. For them, it's a task to be accomplished and then crossed off the list. In Chapter 14, we'll take a look at the importance of maintaining your estate plan to make sure it will continue to function the way you need it to. In order to be effective, the estate plan should be monitored on a regular basis, and updated and maintained as needed.

## What Is Your Estate?

When beginning to discuss estate planning, one of the first things that needs to be understood is what is included in your "estate." When you have a better understanding of what your estate includes, you can design an estate plan that better addresses the issues surrounding that estate. The best planning for a $50,000 estate will likely be different from the best planning for an estate of $5 million. Without knowing what your "estate" is, your planning may not be appropriate.

Your "estate" includes any property that you own or control that has a monetary value. It's the gross value of all of the assets that would be received by your beneficiaries upon your passing. At this point of the discussion, it doesn't matter *how* the beneficiaries would receive the assets (for example, whether the assets are subject to Probate, or have beneficiary designations, or are in a Trust). The "estate" is everything your beneficiaries will receive, from any source and through any process. This would include the following kinds of assets:

- **Real Estate** - your home and any other real estate you own, such as commercial properties, rental homes, vacation homes, vacant lots, and condominiums;

- **Bank Accounts** - any bank accounts, including checking, savings, certificates of deposit, and money market accounts;

- **Retirement Accounts** - any retirement accounts that you own, including 401(k) plans, 403(b) plans, IRA's, and other such retirement plans;

- **Investment Accounts** - any non-retirement investment accounts, including mutual funds, stock accounts and bond accounts;

- **Businesses** - any business interests that you own, whether it's set up as a corporation, a partnership, a Limited Liability Company, or a sole proprietorship;

- **Stocks and Bonds** - any individual stocks or bonds you own (where they are not owned in an investment account, but you actually have the certificates in your possession);

- **Annuities** - any annuities you own;

- **Vehicles** - any vehicles you own, including any automobiles, boats, and RVs;

- **Life Insurance** - any life insurance that you own.

Whenever I begin the process of talking with people about their estate planning, one of the first things we do is get an estimate of the total value of their estate. For some people, this is the first time they have gone through such an exercise, and they are often surprised at how large their estate is.

Figure 1.1 is an estate calculator worksheet, a tool that you can use to estimate the total value of your own estate. I encourage you to go through the process of estimating your estate on the Worksheet. You may be surprised at the result. While it's not necessary at the beginning planning stages to have any exact amounts for the value of your assets, you should try to be as close as possible in estimating the values.

## The Estate Planning Process

The last issue to understand before we dive into the different types of estate plans is a discussion of the different phases of the estate planning process. When done correctly, there are five critical phases to the estate planning process.

1. **Education.** Just as you are beginning to learn more about estate planning and the issues surrounding estate planning, it's important to get a firm understanding of the issues and options available to you in designing your estate plan. If you don't know what options are available to you and the consequences of choosing one option over another, you can't make the best estate plan for you. Getting a solid education in the estate planning basics is critical.

2. **Design.** Once you understand the estate planning options and issues, you will design your estate plan to fit your individual needs and circumstances. This is the phase where you make all of the decisions about how your assets will be handled and managed for you if you become incapacitated, who will help you if that occurs, and how your assets will be handled upon your passing, as well as who will be in charge of that process. The design phase is when you customize your plan to your exact specifications.

3. **Documentation.** In this phase, the legal documents for your estate plan are created. Your estate planning attorney will prepare all of the legal documents that contain the important provisions for your customized plan, just as you designed it. The legal documents may include powers of attorney, a will, a revocable living trust, and health care directives, or a combination of any or all of these.

4. **Implementation.** While designing your plan calls for creative solutions to address your planning needs, implementing the plan relies on strong legal drafting and organizational skills. In the implementation phase, the legal documents that have been prepared are presented to you for review and signature, and then your assets are aligned to coordinate with your planning documents. That could include changing ownership of certain assets to a trust and changing beneficiary designations. Without having your assets properly aligned with your planning, the whole thing could fail to achieve your objectives.

5. **Maintenance.** As mentioned previously, estate planning is a process and a plan needs to be maintained over time to make sure it will continue to operate as intended. You

may have heard the saying, "The only thing constant in life is change." That's painfully true. As life changes, as your assets change, as your family changes, as your goals change, as your finances change, and as the laws affecting your estate plan change, your estate plan must be adjusted as well. Estate plan maintenance is discussed in more detail in Chapter 14.

## Wrapping It Up

As we've seen in this chapter, estate planning isn't just for the wealthy, and it's not just about what happens when you die. It's not a one-time event either.

Everyone who has some assets and who has people or causes they care about needs to do some kind of estate planning. The estate planning tools to be used will depend on their specific situation. In the next five chapters, we'll look more closely at the different planning tools and strategies and see how they work (or don't work) to achieve your planning goals.

# Figure1.1
## Estate Calculator Worksheet

*You may not think that you have much of an estate to plan for. You therefore might not feel that creating a comprehensive estate plan is important. However, most people underestimate the size of their estates, and they consequently underestimate the importance of good estate planning. This worksheet can be useful for you to estimate the current size of your estate.*

**ASSETS** *Approximate Value*

Real Estate: _____
Bank Accounts (*checking, savings, etc.*):_____
Mutual Funds: _____
Stocks and Bonds: _____
Annuities: _____
Retirement Plans (*401(k), IRA, etc.*): _____
Business Interests: _____
Autos, Boats, etc.: _____
Life Insurance: _____
TOTAL ASSETS : _____

**LIABILITIES**

Real Estate Mortgage: _____
Auto Loans: _____
Other Debt: _____
TOTAL LIABILITIES: _____

**TOTAL ESTATE** (*Assets minus Liabilities*) _____

*By going through the process of estimating the total size of your estate, you will be better able to evaluate the kind of estate planning that will meet your needs and goals.*

# Chapter 2

# *No Plan*

E ven if you don't have a written estate plan, you have a plan. The State of Ohio has formulated a plan for those people who die "intestate," which means "without a written estate plan." Ohio Revised Code section 2105.06, known as the "statute of descent and distribution," sets forth the rules for who receives the property of a person who dies intestate.

The distribution of property from an intestate estate is sometimes a very complicated matter, and it's determined solely by who the "closest living relatives" of the deceased person (also called the "decedent") are. To better understand the way this statute works, we'll look at some examples as we go. Here are five of the possible *eleven* different scenarios that could arise in an intestate estate:

**Scenario 1.** If the decedent has children but no surviving spouse, the property will be divided equally among the children of the decedent.

## *Example 1*

    **Facts:** *Tom dies intestate with no spouse and 2 children, Anna and Bruce. He has a total net estate (the value of his assets after all debts are paid) of $200,000.*

**Result:** *Anna and Bruce will each receive an equal share ($100,000).*

**Scenario 2.** If there is a <u>surviving spouse</u> and <u>one or more children</u> of the decedent or their lineal descendants surviving, **and** all of the decedent's <u>children are also children of the surviving spouse</u>, then all of the property goes to the surviving spouse.

## *Example 2*

**Facts:** *Tom dies intestate and leaves behind his wife Mary and 2 children, Anna and Bruce. Mary is the mother of both of Tom's children. He has a total net estate (the value of his assets after all debts are paid) of $200,000.*

**Result:** *Mary receives the entire $200,000.*

It's been fairly straight-forward so far, but hang on now. Here's where it starts to get a little complicated.

**Scenario 3.** If there is a <u>surviving spouse</u> and <u>one child</u> of the decedent, **but** the surviving <u>spouse isn't the natural or adoptive parent of the decedent's child</u>, then the first $20,000 plus one-half of the balance of the estate goes to the surviving spouse, and the remainder goes to the decedent's child.

## *Example 3*

**Facts:** *Tom dies intestate and leaves behind his wife Mary and 1 child, Anna. Mary isn't Anna's mother. He* *has a total net estate (the value of his assets after all debts are paid) of $200,000.*

**Result:** *Mary receives the first $20,000 of the estate, plus one-half of the remaining $180,000 ($90,000), for a total of $110,000. Anna receives the other $90,000.*

**Scenario 4.** If there is a <u>surviving spouse</u> and <u>more than one child</u> of the decedent, and if the <u>spouse is the natural or adoptive parent of at least one but not all of the children</u>, then the first $60,000 of the estate goes to the surviving spouse, plus one-third of the balance of the estate to the spouse, and the remainder to the children equally.

## *Example 4*

**Facts:** *Tom dies intestate and leaves behind his wife Mary and 2 children, Anna and Bruce. Mary isn't Anna's mother, but she is Bruce's mother. Tom has a total net estate (the value of his assets after all debts are paid) of $200,000.*

**Result:** *Mary receives the first $60,000 of the estate, plus one-third of the remaining $140,000 ($46,667), for a total of $106,667. Anna and Bruce split the remaining two-thirds ($93,333), and receive $46,667 each.*

**Scenario 5.** If there is a <u>surviving spouse</u> and <u>more than one child</u> of the decedent, **and** if the <u>spouse isn't the natural or adoptive parent of any of the decedent's children</u>, then the first $20,000 of the estate goes to the surviving spouse, plus one-third of the balance of the estate to the spouse, and the remainder to the children equally.

## Example 5

**Facts:** *Tom dies intestate and leaves behind his wife Mary and 2 children, Anna and Bruce. Mary isn't the mother of either Anna or Bruce. Tom has a total net estate (the value of his assets after all debts are paid) of $200,000.*

**Result:** *Mary receives the first $20,000 of the estate, plus one-third of the remaining $180,000 ($60,000), for a total of $80,000. Anna and Bruce split the remaining two-thirds ($120,000), and receive $60,000 each.*

# Problems with the "No Plan" Approach

The primary problem with not having a written estate plan is that you have no control over how your assets are handled. They are distributed based on the law, as it's applied to your family situation. Your wishes are not taken into consideration at all.

Years ago I helped a woman administer the estate of her deceased husband. He had been married before and had two children from that marriage, and he didn't have any children with my client (this is like "Scenario 5" above). After they were married, he told her that he wanted her to receive all of his property when he passed away, since he didn't have a good relationship with his children and *didn't want them to receive anything.* He refused to make out an estate plan though, thinking that all of his property would all go to his wife because they were married.

The end result in this estate was that my client, the surviving spouse, received the home and their joint bank accounts (more on this when we discuss joint ownership in Chapter 3), and the decedent's retirement account and life insurance (more on this in Chapter 4), but the remaining assets (about $400,000 worth) had to be divided between the surviving spouse and the decedent's two children. Because he had no formal plan controlling those assets, Ohio law controlled them. He didn't want his children to receive anything, but they ended up receiving about *$125,000 each*. Because he didn't have an effective plan, his wishes weren't carried out.

In addition to losing control over your property, when you don't have a formal estate plan you have these problems as well:

- **Probate** – an intestate estate must be administered in Probate Court, and is therefore subject to the "Pitfalls of Probate" discussed in Chapter 9. At this point, we'll simply say that Probate is an expensive, public process that limits your ability to protect your loved ones and control your property. When an intestate estate is in Probate, these issues are even worse than normal.

- **Increased Expenses** – an intestate estate is more expensive to administer than a "normal" Probate estate. The person applying for the authority to handle the estate (called an "Administrator" in this case) must post a Bond in order to be appointed by the Court. A Bond is essentially an "insurance policy" that protects the estate from the Administrator. If the Administrator would run off with the assets, instead of giving them as directed by the law, then the bond would reimburse the estate for the amount stolen. The cost for the Bond is a one-time premium, paid up-front, and is based on the value of the assets in the estate. It's a cost paid out of the estate assets, not by the Administrator personally. A Bond premium can run between several hundred and several thousand dollars (this is in addition to the other expenses and fees associated with Probate).

- Compare this to a testate estate, one where the decedent had a Will or a Trust. When you make out a Will or a Trust, you appoint the people who you trust to do the job right, and the Bond requirement is almost always waived. There's no need for them to buy an insurance policy to protect against the possibility of them stealing.

## Wrapping It Up

A good way of looking at the "No Plan" approach to estate planning is the cliché, "Failing to Plan is Planning to Fail." You lose control over how your assets will be distributed, subject your estate to the Pitfalls of Probate, and by not having a Will, the usual Pitfalls are made even worse.

In our next four Chapters, we're going to take a look at four different ways to maintain some control over the way your assets are distributed (at least better than with No Plan). They each have their positives and negatives. As you read though them, think about your own estate and how you are currently using these different planning methods, or how they could be used for you.

# Chapter 3

# *Joint Ownership with Right of Survivorship*

The next estate planning tool we need to examine is joint ownership with right of survivorship. You're probably already familiar with joint ownership, at least to some degree, and you might already own some assets jointly with another person. You may be surprised to learn that it's an estate planning tool.

Joint ownership occurs when more than one person is the owner of a piece of property. It can occur with any type of property, including real estate, bank accounts, and investment accounts. Most commonly, joint ownership with right of survivorship is seen in two different types of situations:

- when spouses own property together, such as when spouses own their home or bank accounts together; and

- when a parent and a child or children own property together.

You probably have already figured out from the name that with property owned in "survivorship," when one of the owners dies, the deceased owner's interest in the property passes to the surviving owners. It's not necessary to go through any court proceedings in order to transfer the deceased owner's interest in the property to the surviving owners. Let's look at that in operation by looking at a couple of examples.

In this first example, the real estate is owned by a married couple:

## Example 1

*Bob and Mary, husband and wife, own their home jointly with right of survivorship. When Bob dies, Mary automatically receives Bob's ownership interest in the home and becomes the sole owner of the home.*

*A Probate proceeding isn't required to transfer Bob's interest to Mary. All that is required is the recording of an "Affidavit of Survivorship" and Bob's death certificate with the office of the local County Recorder.*

This example shows how joint ownership works with a bank account:

## Example 2

*Mary and her daughter Jane are listed as the owners of a bank account at Local Bank. When Mary passes away, Jane will be the sole owner of this account.*

*A Probate proceeding isn't required to transfer the account to Jane. All that would be required is the presentation of Mary's death certificate to Local Bank.*

In both of the above examples, we see that the property passed to the surviving owner without any need for court proceedings. At first glance, this may make joint ownership seem like a great estate planning tool, since many people list "Avoid Probate" as one of their estate planning goals.

## Shortcomings of Joint Ownership

While owning property jointly with right of survivorship may avoid Probate, it may not be the best way to accomplish this goal. Let's take a look at three different very real scenarios where how joint ownership can go wrong and frustrate a person's planning goals, making things *worse than Probate*.

### *Scenario 1*
### *"The Survivorship Trap"*

*Bob and Mary own their home, jointly with right of survivorship. They are told that this form of ownership will avoid Probate. When Bob dies, Mary receives Bob's interest in the home without any Probate proceedings. The next year, Mary dies. At that time, Mary is the only owner of the property, and a Probate proceeding is therefore needed to transfer Mary's interest in the home to her beneficiaries.*

This is a very common mistake married couples make with their jointly-owned property, thinking it's a "Probate avoidance" tool. It's actually a "Probate delay" tool. While the joint ownership kept the home out of Probate when Bob passed away, it didn't keep the home out of Probate when Mary passed away.

## Scenario 2
## "The one who dies last wins"

Bob and Mary own their home, jointly with right of survivorship. Their goal is to have their home divided equally among their three children when both Bob and Mary have passed away.

Mary dies first, and Bob becomes the sole owner of the house.

A few years later, Bob gets married to a woman named Susan, and because he wants to make sure that Susan has a place to live for the rest of his life if he should die before her, he adds her as a joint owner of the house.

The next year, Bob dies, and Susan becomes the sole owner of the house.

When Susan passes away, her estate plan leaves all of her property, including the house she received from Bob, to her four children. Bob and Mary's three children, who were originally supposed to receive of the House, will receive nothing.

## Scenario 3
## "We thought this would simplify things"

Mary and her daughter Jane are the joint owners of a bank account at Local Bank. When Mary opened the account, Jane went with her to help, and the bank *representative suggested that Jane be added to the account so that she could help Mary with the account management, and so that the account would avoid Probate. Mary's other two daughters are not listed on the account.*

*When Mary passes away, Jane simply has to present Mary's death certificate to the bank, and she will then be the sole owner of the account. Jane doesn't have to divide the account with her sisters, even if the rest of Mary's estate plan states that everything is to be divided equally. In this situation, the joint ownership by-passes any other estate planning that Mary had created.*

Years ago I met with a woman whose mother had recently passed away. When the daughter came to me and asked for my help with her mother's estate, we started by looking at what assets her mother had owned, and how they were owned. The mother had been divorced and remarried, and we discovered that all of her mother's assets had been put into joint ownership with her new husband. Her home, her bank accounts, and her investment accounts were all jointly owned between her and her new husband.

Just a few years before she had died, the mother had prepared a Will leaving all of her assets to her daughter. However, because of the joint ownership, all of her assets avoided Probate and weren't controlled by the Will. The new husband was the sole owner of all of the assets. I was sorry to tell the daughter that she was not legally entitled to any of her mother's assets.

# Wrapping it Up

Joint ownership can be a great way to own property and simplify the transfer of property from a deceased owned to the surviving owner(s). With survivorship tenancy, Probate can be avoided, but you need to be careful that you maintain control over your property at the same time. While avoiding Probate is a great goal, it needs to be done in a way that accomplishes your other goals as well, including making sure that your beneficiaries receive the property.

# Chapter 4

# *Beneficiary Designations*

A nother common tool used in estate planning is beneficiary designations. Once again, most people are very familiar with this tool, as it's used in many different types of situations. We see beneficiary designations most frequently used in life insurance, retirement accounts, and annuities. However, this tool can also be used with real estate, bank accounts, investment accounts, vehicles and securities. In this chapter, we'll examine the specifics of the different uses and evaluate this tool to determine when it can be an effective estate planning option.

## Avoiding Probate

As with joint ownership, beneficiary designations can be used to avoid the Probate process. If an asset has a beneficiary designation, when the owner dies all that is required is the presentation of the owner's death certificate and - in some cases - supporting documentation. The asset will be transferred automatically to the beneficiary or beneficiaries.[1] This is done without the needing to obtain a court order or going through formal court proceedings. For this reason, using beneficiary designations appeals to many people as a simple way of

---

1 For the rest of this chapter, I'll refer to "the beneficiary" for the sake of brevity. In any case, a person can name more than one beneficiary, but I think that if I write "the beneficiary or beneficiaries" every time, it will drive us both crazy.

avoiding Probate. As we'll see later in this chapter, however, using beneficiary designations may not always achieve all of your planning goals.

# Life Insurance

Life insurance is certainly one of the most familiar assets with a beneficiary designation. When a person takes out a life insurance policy on themselves, they are the "insured" (the life controlling the policy), and they generally become the owner of the policy as well. The owner of the policy is given the power to name the beneficiary of the policy. The beneficiary is the person that the death benefit of the policy will be paid to when the insured passes away. The owner can name a primary beneficiary and contingent beneficiaries (beneficiaries who will receive the death benefit if the primary beneficiary isn't living when the insured dies), and can also name multiple people in each category (for example, "to my children in equal shares" can be used as a beneficiary designation).

When the insured dies, the beneficiary completes a claim form and submits the form to the insurance company along with the insured's death certificate. The insurance company then pays the death benefit to the beneficiary. If the primary beneficiary isn't living, then the contingent beneficiary submits the death certificates of the insured and of the primary beneficiary.

# Retirement Accounts and Annuities

Many people are familiar with retirement accounts. These may be 401(k) or 403(b) plans through your employer, or they may be an IRA (either a "Traditional" IRA or a "Roth" IRA). When these accounts are opened, the account owner names a beneficiary to receive the account when the owner dies. When the owner dies, the beneficiary completes a claim form and submits the form to the company along with the owner's death certificate. The company then transfers the account to the beneficiary.

An annuity is an investment product issued by an insurance company. When the annuity is purchased, the owner usually becomes the "annuitant" (the measuring life for the annuity), and they name a beneficiary for the annuity. When the annuitant passes away, the beneficiary completes a claim form and submits the form to the insurance company along with the owner's death certificate, and the rights to the annuity will pass to the beneficiary.[2] This could be paid as a lump sum of money, or as a continuing stream of monthly payments, depending on the specifics of the annuity.

## T.O.D. and P.O.D.

Less common forms of beneficiary designations are the "transfer on death" (T.O.D.) and the "pay on death" (P.O.D.) designations.

The Transfer on Death designation can be used with real estate, motor vehicles and securities in Ohio. For real estate, Ohio law allows a property owner to record an affidavit designating that upon the death of the owner, the property should be transferred to the named beneficiary. When the owner of the real estate dies, the surviving beneficiary records an "Affidavit of Survivorship" with the owner's death certificate in the County Recorder's office in the county where the real estate is located. The Affidavit is evidence of the transfer of the decedent's ownership interest to the beneficiary.

---

2 Except in the case of a "Life Annuity," which no longer has any value at the death of the annuitant. You should consult with a licensed insurance agent to learn more about annuities.

A similar process is used with motor vehicles and securities. A vehicle owner may have the title of their vehicle issued with a "transfer on death" designation. When the vehicle owner dies, the beneficiary presents an Affidavit and the owner's death certificate to the County Auto Title office, and a new title will be issued in the beneficiary's name. The owner of stock in a company may have the stock certificate issued with a "transfer on death" designation. When the owner of the stock dies, the beneficiary presents an Affidavit and the owner's death certificate to the stock transfer agent, and a new stock certificate will be issued in the beneficiary's name.

The "Pay on Death" designation operates in the same manner as the "transfer on death" designation but can be used for bank accounts and investment accounts. With these assets, the account owner can designate that the account would be paid to a beneficiary upon her death. When the owner of the account passes away, the surviving POD beneficiary will only have to present the owner's death certificate to the bank or investment company, and the account will be transferred to them.

## Shortcomings of Beneficiary Designations

Because using beneficiary designations avoids Probate, it would appear that this is a valuable tool to be used in estate planning, and in some cases, it is. However, as we acknowledged earlier, there is no "one size fits all", and the use of beneficiary designations in some cases is inappropriate. Let's look at three ways that using beneficiary designations as a "planning short-cut" can miss the mark.

## 1. If your beneficiary doesn't survive you, the asset won't avoid Probate.

*Molly has an investment account with ABC Financial, and names her daughter Jane as the TOD beneficiary. Before Molly passes away, Jane dies, and Molly doesn't name a new beneficiary on her account.*

*When Molly passes away, the account will have to be Probated since the TOD beneficiary isn't alive to claim the account.*

## 2. With beneficiary designations, there is no centralized fund from which to pay expenses and taxes, and no one is "in charge."

As we saw above, assets that have beneficiary designations are distributed directly to the beneficiaries upon the death of the owner and avoid Probate. If the owner names more than one beneficiary on assets as a way to avoid Probate, then this can create real problems with getting the estate administered and getting critical issues taken care of.

In any estate, whether it's a Probate estate or not, there are issues that need to be addressed. For example, final bills, medical expenses, and funeral and burial expenses will need to be paid. In addition, the final income tax return for the decedent will need to be filed and any taxes owed will need to be paid. Someone needs to be given the authority and direction to do these things and needs to be given the funds to pay the final bills and expenses.

If assets are distributed directly to the beneficiaries, then there is no one "in charge," and there is no fund from which to pay all of the expenses.

Let's take another look at the hypothetical we used above, but instead add another beneficiary.

*Molly has an investment account with ABC Financial, and names her daughter Jane and her son William as the TOD beneficiaries of the account. When Molly dies, all of the assets are divided equally between William and Jane. William and Jane present Molly's death certificate to ABC Financial and the balance in the account is divided equally them.*

*Jane, who lives in the same town as Molly, assumes responsibility for wrapping up Molly's affairs and making sure her final bills are paid. She signs the contract for Molly's $9,000 funeral.*

*Jane goes to William and tells him that the funeral expenses were $9,000 and asks him to pay half. He refuses. Even though he received half of the assets, he has no obligation to pay half of the bills. Jane will have to pay that expense out of the money that she received, without a contribution from William.*

I've met with a large number of families who thought that using TOD designations would not end up being a problem because "everyone gets along" and "they'll just figure it out." In some of these situations, it all worked out just fine, but in a number of them (much too large of a number, in my opinion), the situation turned sour. Here are some of the problems that can develop with this approach:

- One of the beneficiaries doesn't agree to contribute his or her share;

- One of the beneficiaries agrees to contribute, but then doesn't;

- None of the beneficiaries agree to be the one responsible for paying the expenses and taxes (for fear of being the one left holding the bag);

Before you think that this couldn't happen to your family because "everyone gets along," just remember that in every situation where conflicts among beneficiaries develop, all of those people felt that it couldn't happen to them either. I've seen too many times where money changes people or brings out issues from deep in their childhoods (especially sibling rivalries and jealousies).

## 3. You can't protect your beneficiaries when using beneficiary designations.

When assets are distributed to a beneficiary using a beneficiary designation, there's no way to control how and when the distribution is made and no way to protect the beneficiaries. Beneficiary designations result in an "outright distribution" to the beneficiary (the assets are simply turned over to the beneficiary to use however they wish). Sometimes that can be OK. Sometimes it's not. We'll discuss protecting beneficiaries in a lot more detail in Chapter 12, but for now let's look at just a couple of examples.

*Molly is a single mother and has her son John as the beneficiary of her life insurance. John is 16 years old. Molly dies unexpectedly, and John is the recipient of her life insurance death benefit. The life insurance company will pay the death benefit to John, but since*

*John is still a minor, they must have a Guardianship of the Estate established for John to manage the funds. This Guardianship is through the local Probate Court, so even though life insurance doesn't usually need a Court to make the transfer, a Probate Court proceeding is required in this case.*

*As an added drawback, when John reaches the age of 18, the funds in the Guardianship are distributed to him, with no restrictions, guidance or protection.*

For more information on estate planning when you have minor children, please read Chapter 15.

*Molly has all of her assets set up with POD and TOD designations with her daughter Jane as the sole beneficiary. Jane has always struggled with money and with making good decisions about investments and spending.*

*When Molly dies, all of her assets are transferred directly to Jane without Probate. However, since Jane is the sole owner of all of the assets now, she is free to do anything she wants with them. She makes poor spending and investing decisions, and within a year, most of the assets Jane inherited from Molly are gone.*

## Wrapping it Up

In some cases, beneficiary designations work to achieve your planning goals. Other times they fail. This isn't one of those methods that will *always* work or *always* fail. Whether using this tool will work for you depends on your assets, your family situation, your beneficiaries, and your planning needs and goals. In our scenarios above, we saw that the beneficiary designations didn't work when the beneficiary died before the account owner, when one of the beneficiaries wasn't willing to cooperate with the others, when the beneficiary was too young, and when the beneficiary was not good with financial issues. You should consult with an experienced estate planning attorney to discuss your situation to see how beneficiary designations can fit into your specific planning needs and goals.

# Chapter 5

# *Wills*

P robably the most common estate planning tool is the Last
   Will and Testament, commonly referred to as a Will. In
our experience, when people first think about doing estate
planning, they think that they need to do a Will. Typically, this
is simply because they are not familiar with the other types of
estate plans and are not familiar with the issues affecting their
estate planning.

A Will is a written document stating the person's wishes
about the handling of their estate after their death. A Will
generally does two or three things:

- First, it states how the person's property should be
  distributed upon their death, naming the beneficiaries
  of the estate and who should receive what property.

- Second, it appoints the people who would be in charge
  of the Probate estate, referred to as Executor or Personal
  Representative.

- Third, if the Testator (the person making the Will) has
  minor children, the Will also names the people who
  would be appointed the Guardian of the minor children.

# The "Typical Will"

If you are married and have children, I'm pretty sure I already know what your Will says (assuming you already have a Will). I've seen thousands of Wills that people have asked me to review. Almost all of them say something like this:

> *When I die, I leave all of my assets to my spouse, if my spouse is then living. If my spouse isn't living, then I leave all of my assets to my children, in equal shares.*

If you are not married and have children, then your Will probably says something like this:

> *Upon my death I leave all of my assets to my children, in equal shares.*

The plans I quoted above are what we would call "Mom and Dad wills" or a Traditional Will Plan. Probably 98% of the Wills that we review say something very similar to these. In most of these cases, we find that the Wills were created that way because the clients didn't know there were other, better options available to them.

# A Myth about Wills

Often, people will meet with me for an initial consultation and are surprised to learn that the Will they did many years earlier won't keep their estate out of Probate. They believed that by doing a Will, they were taking the steps needed to avoid Probate. They are also surprised to learn that the Will doesn't control the disposition of all of their property.

The truth is that the Will doesn't do anything until it's admitted to Probate. It doesn't control any property while a person is alive, and it only controls property once a person has died and their Probate estate has been opened. It also only controls the property that is "subject to Probate." For example, it won't control any property that is jointly owned with someone else, or property that has a beneficiary designation.

The primary question in determining whether property will be controlled by a Will is whether there is a joint owner or a beneficiary designation. If not, a Probate proceeding will be required. We'll discuss Probate in more detail in Section 2.

## Shortcomings of Will Plans

As with beneficiary designation plans, a Will-based estate plan will work for some people, and will fail for others. Your personal situation will determine whether a Will plan is right for you.

Primarily, a Will plan is inappropriate for those people who want to avoid Probate. As we noted earlier, a Will doesn't avoid Probate, but rather guarantees it for certain kinds of property.

In addition, a Will plan is inappropriate for people who have beneficiaries they want or need to protect. With a Will, the assets are distributed directly to the beneficiary, without any protection or ongoing help. For some beneficiaries, this plan of distribution is inappropriate. We'll look more closely at beneficiary protections in Chapter 12.

## Naming a Guardian

Parents who have minor children use their Wills to nominate the person or persons they would want to serve as the Guardian for their minor children in case the parents die when the children are still minors. Many times, this is the hardest part of the estate planning process for parents. Who can they name as the Guardians? This is an extremely important decision, and sometimes the answer is hard to come by. Chapter 15 includes my four-step process for picking a Guardian for your kids.

## Cost of Will Plans

Many people are drawn to Will-based estate plans because of the cost. The initial cost of setting up a Will plan is generally lower than other alternatives (like a Living Trust). However, the lower initial cost of the Will plan is generally offset by the higher overall cost of the Will plan, when the cost of a Probate proceeding is taken into account. We'll look at the costs associated with Probate in Chapter 8. In many cases, using a Will as the foundation of your estate plan is being penny-wise and pound-foolish. Before you make your decision, make sure you examine all of the costs associated with your estate plan; not just the initial cost of setting up the plan, but also the cost of administering your estate with the planning tool you choose.

## Wrapping it Up

A Will plan is the most familiar type of estate planning for most people, and as a result it's the initial default plan a lot of people go to. However, for a lot of people the Will plan may not be the most appropriate. If you want to avoid Probate or if you want to protect your beneficiaries, then a Will plan is something you'll want to avoid.

# Chapter 6

# *Revocable Living Trusts*

The last type of type of estate plan we need to look at here is a Revocable Living Trust. We have found living trusts to be the most effective tool for planning most of our client's estates, giving them the flexibility to deal with whatever issues they have and helping them meet their planning goals.

Many people aren't familiar with trusts and how they work. Sometimes people think that a trust is a very complicated legal instrument, and something they could never understand, and certainly would never need. This isn't true. Simply stated, a trust is a type of Will substitute. Like a Will, a trust generally does two things:

- First, it states how the person's property should be distributed upon their death, naming the beneficiaries of the estate and who should receive what property.

- Second, it appoints the people who would be in charge of the Trust property when the Trustmaker isn't able, referred to as Successor Trustee.

However, unlike a Will, a trust avoids Probate, goes into much more detail about how the property should be used, and allows for opportunities for protecting beneficiaries.

# Understanding Trusts

We'll go into a LOT more detail on trusts in Section 3 of this Book. For now, let's just look at the basics to get an initial understanding of what trusts are and how they can be used to meet your planning goals.

## *The Parties*

Let's start our discussion on trusts by looking at who the three parties of every trust are:

- *Trustmaker*: a person who creates a revocable living trust. The Trustmaker is also sometimes referred to as a Settlor, Grantor, or Trustor.

- *Trustee:* the person named in a trust to be in charge of the trust assets. The Trustee is responsible for making all investment and distribution decisions for the trust assets. The Trustee follows the instructions from the Trustmaker written in the trust document and uses the trust assets for the benefit of the trust beneficiaries.

- *Beneficiaries:* the people the trust is designed to benefit.

## *What a Trust is*

A trust is an agreement between the Trustmaker and the Trustee for the management of the trust property for the benefit of the trust beneficiaries. In most cases, when a Revocable Living Trust is created, the Trustmaker names himself or herself as the initial Trustee, and also names himself or herself as the beneficiary. Thus, the trust is initially an agreement between a person and herself for the use of her property for her own needs. When the trust is first created, the Trustmaker remains in control of their property, retaining all control and authority over everything.

## Wills and Trusts - Compared

As I mentioned earlier, a Trust can be considered a "Will Substitute" since it does some of the same things that a Will does. It states who will receive a person's property when they die, and it appoints the people who will be in charge of the trust administration when the Trustmaker is no longer able to manage their own property. However, there are several significant differences between Wills and Trusts:

- A Trust controls a person's property during their lifetime, so that if they become incapacitated, the Trust will be used to continue to provide for their needs. A Will doesn't have any control during a period of incapacity – only at death.

- A Trust will avoid Probate for all assets that are owned by the Trust at the time the Trustmaker passes away. Remember that Probate is needed if a person has assets without a joint owner or a beneficiary designation. A Trust avoids Probate when the Trustmaker's assets are transferred into the trust. Wills only work in Probate.

- Trusts can be used to protect beneficiaries by structuring how the inheritance is administered for the beneficiaries. With Wills, the assets are distributed directly to the beneficiaries, which may be inappropriate for some beneficiaries. Chapter 12 covers beneficiary protections in more detail.

# Wrapping it Up

A Living Trust can be the most versatile and useful estate planning tool for many people. It can be used to achieve your planning goals, including avoiding Probate, protecting beneficiaries, streamlining your estate administration and simplifying the estate process. In Section 3 of this book we'll go deeper into trusts to see the specifics about how trusts work and how they are used to plan your estate.

# Section 2

## *Probate*

P robate is a process of administering a person's property through the state court system when they can't manage their own property, either because they have become incapacitated or they have passed away. Probate administration is done in the Ohio Probate Courts under the supervision and authority of the Probate Court judges.

# Chapter 7

# *What is Probate?*

P robate is the process of administering a person's estate through the court system. It's needed in situations when individuals can't take care of themself or their property and Court authority is needed to empower someone else to do those things for them. There are two types of Probate proceedings: a living Probate (better known as a "Guardianship") and a death Probate (better known as an Estate Administration).

## Guardianships

A Guardianship is needed when a person is legally incompetent and is therefore not capable of managing their personal affairs and/or their financial affairs. If an incompetent person isn't capable of managing their personal affairs (meaning they are not capable of making decisions about their own well-being), then a "Guardianship of the Person" is needed. If an incompetent person isn't capable of managing their property or financial affairs, then a "Guardianship of the Estate" is needed.

# Guardianship of the Person

A Guardianship of the Person is required if an incompetent person isn't capable of managing their personal affairs. This is used in two different circumstances. First, it's used for a minor who has no parents. Second, it's used for an incompetent adult.

The role of the Guardian of the Person is to protect and control the person of the Ward (the incompetent person), to provide suitable living arrangements for them, and to direct their medical care and education. The Guardian of the Person reports to the Probate Court on an annual or biennial basis as directed by the Court on the condition of the Ward, including their living arrangements, any changes in their physical and mental condition, and the care being provided to the Ward.

# Guardianship of the Estate

A Guardianship of the Estate is required if a person is the owner of property and they are not capable of managing that property ("property" includes real estate, bank accounts, investments, etc.). Once again, we see this used for either minor children or incompetent adults. The Guardian of the Estate is given the authority by the Probate Court to take control of the Ward's property and use that property for the Ward's benefit.

The role of the Guardian of the Estate is to use the property of the Ward for the benefit of the Ward. Guardianship funds can only be spent with the

Court's prior approval, and the Guardian is required to keep records of everything that is done with the Ward's property. An Account must be filed annually with the Court showing exactly how the property was used.

# Estate Administration

The other type of Probate, and the one that most people probably think of when they hear the word "Probate," is the Estate Administration when a person dies.

An Estate Administration Probate proceeding is required if a decedent owned assets that must go through Probate. Assets need to go through Probate if the decedent was the sole owner of the asset (there was not a joint owner) and there was not a beneficiary designation for the asset.

For example, if a person owns a house jointly with right of survivorship (see Chapter 3) and that person dies, no Probate would be required because the house would transfer automatically to the surviving joint owner. However, when the surviving joint owner dies, at that point there is no other joint owner on the property, so the house would have to go through Probate.

The purpose of an Estate Administration proceeding is to provide a legal process for the handling of the deceased person's assets. The Probate Court empowers a person (called an Executor or Administrator, depending on whether the decedent left a Will or not) to take control of the decedent's property and administer it. The Executor or Administrator is responsible for payment of all debts of the decedent and the distribution of the decedents remaining assets to the decedent's beneficiaries or heirs.

Think about selling a house, for example. If my wife and I are going to sell our house, then our signatures will be needed on the Deed in order to transfer title to our buyer. If we are both deceased and our house needs to be sold, someone stills needs to sign a Deed to transfer the house to the buyer. If we own the house in our names (not in a trust), then a Probate proceeding will be needed in order for the house to be sold. The Probate Court would appoint someone to be the Executor of the estate and will give that person the legal authority to access and control the assets of the estate. Included in that authority would be the authority to sign a Deed on behalf of the estate to sell the house.

## Wrapping it Up

At its essence, Probate is needed to give legal authority to someone to manage someone else's person or someone else's assets and to oversee the management process. It's needed when other arrangements haven't been made to avoid the process.

# Chapter 8

# *The Probate Process*

I t's helpful at this point to talk a little bit about the Probate
process. I mentioned in the last chapter that there are two
types of Probate proceedings, a living Probate (Guardianship)
and a death Probate (Estate Administration). In this chapter,
we'll look only at the process of the Estate Administration.

## Types of Probate Estate Proceedings

There are three types of estate Probate proceedings, and
the proceeding needed for a particular estate depends on the
amount of assets in the Probate estate. The three types are:

- A Summary Release from Administration;

- A Relief from Administration; and

- A " Full Probate"

## *Summary Release from Administration*

The Summary Release from Administration procedure is
available only for very small estates. An estate qualifies for the
Summary Release procedure if the value of the Probate assets
is the lesser of $5,000 or the amount of the funeral and burial

expenses. That sounds a little confusing at first, but it helps to see some examples.

> *Sam dies and the only asset that needs to go through probate is a bank account with $4,500 in it. Sam's funeral and burial expenses totaled $6,000.*

> *Sam's estate qualifies for the Summary Release procedure because the estate assets are less than $5,000 and less than the funeral and burial expenses.*

> *Sam dies and the only asset that needs to go through probate is a bank account with $6,500 in it. Sam's funeral and burial expenses totaled $9,000.*

> *Sam's estate doesn't qualify for the Summary Release procedure because the estate assets are more than $5,000.*

In the Summary Release procedure, the Applicant is the person who paid or is responsible for paying the funeral and burial expenses. The Applicant applies for the Summary Release, showing the amount of the Probate assets and the funeral and burial expenses. The Court then orders that the estate assets be distributed to the Applicant, either to reimburse the Applicant for the expenses or to allow the Applicant to pay the expenses.

The Summary Release procedure is much faster and easier than a Full Probate, usually only taking a few weeks to complete.

## *Relief from Administration*

The Relief from Administration procedure is available if either (1) the assets subject to Probate are $35,000 or less, or

(2) the Probate assets are $100,000 or less AND the surviving spouse is entitled to all of the assets.

In the Relief from Administration procedure, an Applicant will file the Application for Relief from Administration, providing the following information to the Probate Court:

- The decedent's Will (if there was a Will);

- The statement of the decedent's heirs at law and the named beneficiaries in the will;

- A statement of the assets and liabilities of the Probate estate;

- The requested disposition of the assets of the estate.

Upon reviewing the Application and related documents, the court will approve the Application for Relief from Administration and will order the disposition of the estate assets as requested in the Application. The distribution of the assets will be according to the decedent's Will, if there was a Will, or according to the laws of descent and distribution (see chapter 2) if there was not a Will.

As with the Summary Release procedure, a Relief from Administration is much faster than a "Full Probate" and usually only takes a few months to complete.

## Full Probate

A Full Probate procedure is, as the name suggests, the entire Probate process without any shortcuts or releases from the full administration process. When people talk about "Probate" and "avoiding Probate" they are usually referring to the Full Probate procedure.

To better understand the Full Probate process, let's take a look at the various steps in the procedure, examining what is required, the timeline, and the information that needs to be provided.

## *Phase 1*

## *The Initial Filing*

To begin the Probate process, an Applicant will file the initial Probate papers. These papers will "open the estate", and include the following:

- the decedent's Will (if there was a Will);

- a statement of the decedent's heirs at law and the beneficiaries named in the Will;

- an estimate of the assets in the estate;

- an Application for authority to administer the estate (to be named the Executor or the administrator of the estate); and

- the Probate Court's orders to (1) admit the Will to Probate; (2) appoint the Executor.

When filing the decedent's Will, notice of the filing must be provided to all of the persons who are "interested" in the estate. Those people who are "interested" in the estate are those people who are named as the beneficiaries in the Will, as well as those people who would be the beneficiaries if the decedent didn't have a Will (the heirs at law). In the initial filing, the Applicant must obtain a signed waiver from all of the interested persons, stating that they do not need or want to receive a written Notice of the filing of the Will from the court. If a waiver isn't obtained from an interested person, the court sends a notice to that person by certified mail. The purpose of the Notice is to give all interested persons an opportunity to contest the will (to claim that it is not valid).

After examining the initial document filing, if everything is in order, the court will issue an Entry admitting the decedent's Will to Probate and will issue "Letters of Authority" to the Applicant, naming him or her as the Executor or the Administrator of the estate. The Letters of Authority gives the Executor the authority to take control of the estate assets, as well as take all necessary and authorized action on behalf of the decedent's estate.

## Phase 2

## The Inventory

The second phase of the Probate proceeding is the identification and valuation of all of the estate assets. This is done in the Inventory of the estate. The Inventory must be filed within 3 months from the date that the estate was opened.

In the Inventory, the Executor must identify all of the estate assets with specificity. This means that the Executor must list all of the assets of the estate that are subject to Probate and provide all information necessary to fully identify those assets. For example, all bank accounts must be identified, with account numbers and balances in each account as of the date of death of the decedent.

Sometimes the value of an asset is readily identifiable, such as with a bank account. You can look at the bank statement and confirm the exact account balance as of a specific date. With other assets, however, the values are not as readily available, and it's necessary in most cases to have those assets appraised. For example, an appraisal is required for real estate or for automobiles. To obtain the appraisal, the Executor must hire an appraiser who has been approved by the Probate Court to conduct Probate appraisals, and have the appraiser provide a written statement of the value of the asset. The appraisal is filed with the Probate Court along with the Inventory.

Once again, it's necessary to provide all of the estate beneficiaries with a copy of the Inventory. The Court will schedule a hearing on the Inventory and give all interested person's notice of the hearing. The beneficiaries can sign a written Waiver of the right to receive this notice from the court (as in the waiver of notice of filing of will). The purpose of this hearing is to give the estate beneficiaries an opportunity to contest the Inventory, either claiming that certain assets weren't listed in the Inventory or that the value of the listed assets is incorrect.

After reviewing the Inventory, and assuming that there are no objections to the Inventory from the beneficiaries, the court will approve the Inventory.

## Phase 3
## The Account

Once the Inventory has been approved, the Executor can start selling estate assets and consolidating the accounts into an estate checking account. When the estate assets are sold, the proceeds of sale are deposited into the estate checking account as well.

The first responsibility of the Executor is to pay all of the valid debts of the decedent and the expenses of the estate administration (for example, the Court's filing fees and the attorney and Executor fees). Once the bills have been paid, as well as the expenses of the estate administration, the remainder of the estate assets is available for distribution to the estate's beneficiaries.

For distribution of the estate assets, certain assets can be distributed "in kind" to the beneficiaries, meaning they are distributed without first being sold. For example, real estate and automobiles can be distributed "in kind" to the beneficiaries, simply by transferring the real estate or automobiles to them. Other times, all of the assets will be sold (including any real estate and automobiles) and the beneficiaries will receive their distribution in the form of a check from the Estate.

The final step of the process is for the Executor to file the Account with the Probate Court. The Account must be filed within 6 months from the opening of the Probate estate. The Account is a statement of what was done with all of the assets of the estate. The Account must show the receipt by the Executor of all assets that were listed in the Inventory, must show the payment of all of the estate's expenses, the decedent's valid debts, and any taxes due, and must show all of the distributions to the beneficiaries. The Account must show an exact amount of receipts and the same exact amount of disbursements, with the Executor accounting for every penny of the estate.

The Executor is required to provide a complete copy of the Account to all of the estate beneficiaries. The Court will once again schedule a hearing on the Account and give all of the estate beneficiaries an opportunity to object to the handling of the estate. After reviewing the Account, and assuming that there are no objections to the Account from the beneficiaries, the Probate Court will approve the Account and close the estate.

# Wrapping it Up

The Probate process is a very specific set of rules and procedures used in the administration of a decedent's estate. It's a complicated system of forms and timelines that families must go through, and as we'll see in the next chapter, it has a lot of drawbacks. After learning about Probate and the alternatives, most people will want to design their estate so that Probate is avoided. We'll examine the reasons why people want to avoid Probate in the next chapter.

# Chapter 9

# *Why Avoid Probate?*

M ost of the people we meet with to discuss estate planning have heard that they want to "avoid Probate." These opinions usually come from one of two categories:

1. People who have been involved in a Probate proceeding and are familiar with its pitfalls;

2. People who have not been involved with Probate before but have heard that it's something they don't want.

Our first job, then, is to determine our client's prior experience level with and understanding of Probate, and make sure that they understand how Probate works, why Probate is required, and why it should be avoided in their situation. In the two previous chapters, we looked at what Probate is for and how it works. In this chapter will examine the "pitfalls of Probate."

Essentially, there are four main problems with Probate. They are as follows:

- Expense;
- Public
- Loss of control; and
- Multiple Probates.

# Probate is Expensive

The primary concern most people have with Probate is the expense associated with this process. The majority of the expense of the Probate process comes from the attorney fee, although this isn't the only expense. Let's look at all of the expenses associated with this process.

## *Court Costs*

In order to file an estate in Probate Court, the applicant must pay the costs set by the Probate Court. The amount of the filing fee depends upon the type of proceeding used. For example, in a Summary Release from Administration proceeding, the court costs for a Lucas County estate would be $95. An estate using the Relief from Administration procedure would have court costs ranging between $90 and $160. In the same county, a Full Probate filing would require an initial court deposit of $350, with additional costs due throughout the proceeding.

## *Appraisal fees*

As we discussed in Chapter 8, if any of the assets of the estate have a value that is "not readily ascertainable," it's necessary to obtain an appraisal for those assets. An appraisal is required for each asset which falls into this category. That could be real estate, automobiles, or collections, such as firearms or antiques or art. The costs to obtain these appraisals will vary and will usually range from $100 to $350 per appraisal.

# Bonding Cost

If a person died without a Will and their estate must go through the Probate process, then there will be an additional expense for their estate. This additional cost is a "bond" for the Administrator.

A bond is essentially an insurance policy insuring the estate against the Administrator running off with the estate assets. With a Will, the requirement for a bond is almost always waived (the person nominated as Executor is trusted to behave properly, so a bond isn't required). However, if there isn't a Will, then bond can't be waived.

The bond is based on the value of the personal property of the estate (everything except any real estate). The cost for the bond will be the premium for the insurance policy and is determined by the insurance company. Depending on the size of the estate, the bond cost could be $1,000 or more.

# Attorney Fees

The above-mentioned costs (court costs, appraisal fees, bond) can add up to several thousand dollars, but the majority of the expense for Probate comes is for the attorney fee. The attorney fee to be charged in Probate is based upon the fee schedule set by each local Probate Court. The local Probate Court rules set the method for determining the amount of attorney fees that can be charged by the attorney for the estate. In these local court rules, the fee is set as a percentage of the assets of the decedent.

For example, in Lucas County, Ohio, the attorney fee is charged as follows:

- 4.5% of the first $100,000 of Probate assets;

- 3.5% of the next $300,000 of Probate assets;

- 2.5% of the balance of the Probate assets; and

- 1.5% of the non-Probate assets in the decedent's taxable estate.

Let's look at a couple of examples of estates to see this attorney fee calculation in practice:

## Example 1

*Joe died as a resident of Lucas County, Ohio with a house valued at $100,000 and a checking account valued at $10,000.*

*The total estate value is $110,000 and the total attorney fee would be $4,850.*

*This is calculated as $4,500 on the first $100,000 of the estate (4.5%), and $350 on the remaining $10,000 (3.5%).*

## Example 2

*Joe died a resident of Lucas County, Ohio. At the time of his death he owned a house valued at $200,000, bank accounts with a total value of $50,000, a $15,000 car, and mutual fund investments valued at $175,000. The total estate value is $440,000, and the total attorney fee*

*to be charged would be $16,000. The fee is calculated*
*as follows:*

> *First $100,000 = $4,500 (4.5%)*
>
> *Next $300,000 = $10,500 (3.5%)*
>
> *Next $40,000 = $1,000 (2.5%)*
>
> *Total Fee  = $16,000*

Given all of the expenses associated with the Probate process, it's easy to see why people try to plan their estates so that Probate is avoided.

## Probate is Public

The next major pitfall of Probate is the fact that a Probate proceeding is public. All of the information contained in a Probate Court record is public and can be viewed by anyone for any purpose. While that may seem to be a small issue at first, when you realize what information is contained in the Probate Court record, the public nature of the proceedings becomes much more of a concern.

### *Parties Involved*

In the initial filing, the names and addresses of all of the persons involved in the estate are filed. This gives anyone a way of contacting any person involved in the estate.

# Inventory

The Inventory is a listing of all of the assets in the estate with their values. That includes bank and investment account numbers and their current values, details on all real estate and vehicles owned, and values of business interests. Would you want that information about you to be made public? When I present educational seminars about estate planning, I will often jokingly ask for a volunteer in the room to stand and tell everyone else a detailed listing of all of their assets, including account numbers and values. In the past 20 years, I haven't gotten a volunteer yet. However, this is exactly the information shown in the Probate Inventory.

# Account

At the end of the estate the Account is filed showing what happened with all of the estate assets. The Account shows how the assets were distributed, including who received which assets and how much was distributed to each beneficiary.

The information that is required to be filed in a Probate proceeding is personal and private, and most people will want to make sure that the information stays out of the public proceedings of Probate.

# Lack of Protections in Probate

The next major problem with Probate is the lack of protections for beneficiaries. The Probate process is designed to make sure that the decedent's creditors are paid and the remaining assets are distributed to the beneficiaries. The process is designed to have estates close as soon as possible without ongoing administration for the estate. In many situations, this isn't the best result for the recipients of the property.

The Probate process generally will have the distributions to the beneficiaries made as "outright" distributions, meaning there is no ongoing administration for those assets once the distribution is made to the beneficiary. For example, for beneficiaries who have little experience handling money, receiving a relatively large sum can be dangerous. They don't have any experience with making the decisions necessary to invest wisely and spend the money they inherit. Their inheritance can be wasted or lost.

The same issues arise for beneficiaries who have creditor issues, or aren't legally able to manage their own finances, or who have marital problems. See Chapter 12 for a more detailed discussion of protecting beneficiaries.

Because of the way Probate is designed to distribute assets to beneficiaries, people will often look to other ways to plan their estate so that they can protect their loved ones.

## More Than One *(Multiple Probates)*

When you consider the pitfalls of Probate, it's clear that in most cases the Probate process should be avoided. However, in some cases, it's even necessary to have multiple Probates. These generally occur in estates where there is real estate in multiple states, or when there are minor beneficiaries.

## Property in other States

If a person who owns real estate in another state, such as a cottage in Michigan or a condo in Florida, then in addition to having a Probate of their Ohio property (their entire estate except for the out-of-state property), they will require an "ancillary proceeding" to administer the out-of-state property.

When there is out-of-state real estate, the state laws of the other state will control how that real estate is administered. The Register of Deeds in the Michigan county where the real estate is located, for example, won't honor the order from the Ohio Probate Court for the transfer of the Michigan property. A Probate proceeding must be opened in the county where the real estate is located for an order from that Court for the transfer of the real estate to the Ohio executor, who can then distribute the real estate to the proper estate beneficiaries. This ancillary Probate proceeding adds additional time, expense, and administrative hassle to the regular Ohio Probate proceeding.

## Minor Beneficiaries

If the beneficiaries of an estate are minors, we've seen how they are not able to own property and how a living Probate (Guardianship) will be required for them. In these cases, the Guardianship for the minor has additional expense and loss of control and lack of protections for the minor beneficiary. The issues associated with Guardianships for minors are discussed more completely in Chapter 15.

## Wrapping it Up

Probate is something that most people want to avoid, and they begin the estate planning process with "Avoiding Probate" as one of their estate planning goals. By avoiding Probate, they are able to reduce the cost associated with administering their estate, maintain privacy, and protect their beneficiaries. In the next chapter we'll look at the different ways you can design your estate plan to avoid Probate.

# Chapter 10

# *Avoiding Probate*

W e saw the "pitfalls of Probate" in the last chapter and explored the reasons why people want to make sure that their estates avoid the Probate process. There are several ways of avoiding Probate, and in doing your estate planning you should explore all of the available options.

## Joint Ownership

As we saw in Chapter 3, assets that are owned jointly with another person will avoid Probate when a joint owner passes away. While this does appear to be a viable estate planning method for avoiding Probate, it's usually inappropriate and ineffective. Here is what we saw in Chapter 3 about the shortcomings of joint ownership:

1. Joint ownership doesn't always avoid Probate, but instead delays it.

2. Joint ownership subjects property to the creditors of all joint owners.

3. You can lose control over the property using joint ownership.

So we've seen that although joint ownership is a way to avoid Probate, it's not entirely effective, and the risks associated with using joint ownership as a way of avoiding Probate are not justified in most circumstances.

## Beneficiary Designations

We saw in Chapter 4 that assets with a beneficiary designation will also avoid Probate, but we also saw that using beneficiary designations to avoid Probate doesn't solve all of the planning issues or meet all of the planning goals. Sometimes using beneficiary designations can create more problems than it solves.

By way of a quick reminder, here are the shortcomings of using beneficiary designations as a means of avoiding Probate:

1. If the named beneficiaries don't survive you, the assets won't avoid Probate.

2. When beneficiary designations are used, there is no centralized fund from which to pay expenses and taxes, and no one is in charge. This can create a situation where disputes break out among your beneficiaries about who should be doing what.

3. You can't protect your beneficiaries with beneficiary designations (see Chapter 12 for more information on protecting beneficiaries).

While using beneficiary designation does avoid Probate (usually), it should only be used in very limited circumstances.

# Living Trusts

Using a living trust is the most effective way of avoiding Probate. In the next four chapters we'll look at how living trusts work, how they avoid Probate, and why they are so beneficial.

# Section 3

## *Living Trusts*

# Chapter 11

# Understanding Revocable Living Trusts

A lot of people choose a Revocable Living Trust as the primary tool for planning their estate. People choose Revocable Living Trusts (RLTs) for a lot of specific reasons, but the main reasons are (1) because they are generally the most effective and efficient way of avoiding Probate and making sure that your estate is administered in accordance with your wishes and (2) with an RLT you can customize the way that property is distributed to your beneficiaries. We looked at why people want to avoid Probate in Chapter 10, and we'll look at protecting your beneficiaries in Chapter 12. We looked very briefly at Living Trusts in Chapter 6, and in this chapter we'll go into more detail about how trusts are designed and why people use them.

## The Basic Parties – a Brief Review

Chapter 6 included a discussion of the parties to a trust. For a refresher and to keep you from having to turn back to that chapter to remember who is who, I'll say it again. Every trust has three types of parties:

- *Trustmaker*: a person who creates a revocable living trust. The Trustmaker is also sometimes referred to as a Settlor, Grantor, or Trustor.

- *Trustee:* the person named in a trust to be in charge of the trust assets. The Trustee is responsible for making all investment and distribution decisions for the trust assets. The Trustee follows the instructions from the Trustmaker written in the trust document, and uses the trust assets for the benefit of the trust beneficiaries.

- *Beneficiary:* the person or persons for whom the trust is written to benefit.

## Written for Three Phases of Life

I stated in Chapter 5 that a Will only operates in Probate Court after a person dies. Unlike a Will, an RLT operates immediately upon its signing, and is therefore written to cover three phases in a person's life:

1. **Alive and Well.** An RLT is first written to operate when the Trustmaker is alive and capable of managing his own financial affairs. In this phase, the Trustmaker will usually serve as the Trustee, and will also be the primary beneficiary. In this phase, the Trustmaker/Trustee has full control over the assets of the trust, and can use them however they want. They make all of the investing decisions, all of the spending decisions, and all of the distribution decisions.

2. **Alive but Incapacitated.** The second phase a trust is written for is the possibility of the Trustmaker becoming incapacitated. This, of course, refers to an incapacity resulting from an illness or injury that renders the Trustmaker unable to "effectively manage his property

and financial affairs." If the situation arises, it will be necessary to have someone manage the trust assets for the benefit of the Trustmaker.

When the trust is designed, additional Trustees are named to manage the trust assets if the Trustmaker becomes incapacitated. These Trustees, called "Successor Trustees," do not have any power or authority unless and until the Trustmaker becomes incapacitated.

The job of a Successor Trustee upon the incapacity of the Trustmaker is to use the trust assets as instructed in the trust. Generally, the instructions are to use the trust assets to continue to provide for the needs of the Trustmaker, as well as anyone else who is dependent on the Trustmaker (for example the Trustmaker's spouse or children).

3. **Upon Death.** The final phase an RLT is written for is the Trustmaker's death. When we design the trust with our clients, we cover several issues for this phase: first, who will be in charge of the assets after the Trustmaker dies (again, called the Successor Trustees); second, who will receive the assets of the trust, and third, how will the assets of the trust be distributed to those beneficiaries. We'll look at the "how" in much more detail in Chapter 12.

# Designing the RLT for the Three Stages of Life

As I showed earlier, there are several parties named in the Trust: the Trustmaker, the Trustee (or Trustees), and the beneficiary (or beneficiaries). The people who fill these roles will be different for each of the stages of the trust.

## Alive and Well Phase

When the RLT is set up, the Trustmaker will generally name himself or herself as the initial Trustee and the primary beneficiary of the RLT. If a couple wants to create a joint trust instead of creating separate trusts for each person (which is the most common way of doing it in recent years), then they will both be the Trustmakers and the initial Co-Trustees and the initial beneficiaries. The Trustmakers can also direct that the trust property should be used for the benefit of anyone else who is dependent on the Trustmakers for support, such as the children of the Trustmakers.

## Alive but Incapacitated Phase

While the Trustmaker is still alive but is incapacitated, they need someone new to serve as the Successor Trustee. Because the Trustmaker is still living, he will remain the beneficiary of the trust. The role of the Successor Trustee upon incapacity is to use the trust assets to provide for the needs of the Trustmaker. This means that he will be managing the Trustmaker's finances and assets to assure that the Trustmaker's needs are being met. This may mean that he is responsible for paying the medical expenses of the Trustmaker, the ongoing living expenses, and any other needs that the Trustmaker has.

If this is a joint trust for a couple, then they will usually say that the other spouse will serve as the sole Trustee if one of them becomes incapacitated. If one is already deceased and then the other becomes incapacitated, then they will name some other trusted person to serve as the Successor Trustee. That could be adult children, siblings, parents, or trusted friends. If none of those choices are appropriate, the Trustmaker could also name a professional Trustee, such as an attorney, a CPA, or a bank or trust company to serve as the Successor Trustee.

## *After Death Phase*

When the Trustmaker or Trustmakers have passed away, the trust then operates for the benefit of the next beneficiaries. When the RLT is initially designed, the Trustmakers make decisions about who will be in charge of the trust (their Successor Trustees) and who the trust will be for the benefit of (their beneficiaries).

- **Successor Trustees upon Death.** When the Trustmaker passes away, the Successor Trustee's responsibility is to manage the trust assets as directed in the trust document. This will generally fall into two categories of responsibility. First, the Successor Trustee must "administer" the Trustmaker's estate, paying their final expenses (funeral bills, medical bills, and any other debts), consolidating the trust assets, and getting the assets of the trust ready for the next phase of administration. Second, the Successor Trustee administers the trust assets for the benefit of the trust beneficiaries. This could mean that the trust assets are distributed directly to those beneficiaries (an "outright distribution"), or there could be ongoing administration of the assets for the benefit of the beneficiaries within the trust. We'll look at the issues surrounding the distribution of assets for the beneficiaries in Chapter 12.

- **Contingent Beneficiaries:** Just as the trust has initial beneficiaries upon its creation, beneficiaries after the Trustmaker has passed away are named at that time as well. They can be done in several different "levels."

- **Primary Beneficiaries.** These are the beneficiaries who are intended to receive the benefit of the trust when the Trustmakers have passed away. For example:

  *"Upon the death of me and my spouse, my property shall be distributed to my children, in equal shares."*

  In this example "my children" are the primary beneficiaries of the trust upon my death.

- **Contingent beneficiaries.** When we are designing the trust, it's important to address the possibility that one or more of the primary trust beneficiaries might not be living when it's time to distribute property to them. We therefore need to name contingent beneficiaries to receive property that had been intended for a primary beneficiary. For example:

  *"Upon the death of me and my spouse, my property shall be distributed to my children, in equal shares. If any of my children predeceases me, then that child's share shall be distributed in equal shares to that child's descendants."*

  In this example, a "deceased child's descendants" are the contingent beneficiaries.

- **Remote contingent beneficiaries.** There is always the possibility that all of the intended beneficiaries (the people that the Trustmaker want their property to go to - usually children, grandchildren, great-grandchildren, etc.) are not living at the time that property is to be distributed. We therefore name "remote contingent beneficiaries" to direct how property would be distributed in that case.

The naming of the remote contingent beneficiaries can be done in several different ways. A Trustmaker can be very specific, naming an individual or group of individuals, or charitable organizations, or a combination of individuals and organizations as the remote contingent beneficiaries. If they don't want to be specific, then the Trustmaker can be very generic, understanding that in most cases, the distributions will go either to the primary beneficiaries or the contingent beneficiaries and won't make it to the remote contingent beneficiary level. The generic remote contingent distribution would be "to my heirs at law," leaving the property to the Trustmaker's closest living relatives according to Ohio law (see Chapter 2 for an explanation of "heirs at law").

## Trusts avoid Probate

Unlike a Will, an RLT can be used to avoid Probate, which makes it a preferred tool for planning an estate. A trust will avoid Probate when the assets of the Trustmaker are transferred into the trust during the Trustmaker's lifetime. This process is sometimes called "funding the trust" (we prefer to call the process "Asset Alignment'). In order to have an estate avoid Probate, all of the assets that would ordinarily otherwise be subject to Probate must be transferred to the trust. This includes all real estate, bank accounts, investment accounts stock, vehicles, business interests, and personal property. We'll look more closely at the Asset Alignment process in Chapter 13.

# RLTs are NOT an Asset Protection Tool

When we are sitting with clients discussing how to plan their estates, we are often asked about how to protect assets from the high cost of long-term care or from other potential creditors. It's generally in the context of whether an RLT will protect their assets from their creditors.

The short answer is "no." Because the RLT is set up to allow the Trustmakers to serve as Trustees, to maintain control over their assets, and to have unlimited access to their assets, their creditors can get at those assets as well. So while an RLT can be set up to provide protections for your beneficiaries, it won't protect your assets from your creditors and potential creditors.

In order to protect your assets from your potential creditors, you have to put them out of your control. That is either done through an outright gift (not recommended), or with an Irrevocable Trust. In an Irrevocable Trust, someone else is named as the Trustee, and the Trustmaker isn't allowed to be given assets from the trust (although sometimes they are designed to give the Trustmaker the right to receive the income from the assets in the Irrevocable Trust). Because the assets can't be given to the Trustmaker, they can't be used to pay the Trustmaker's creditors.

# Wrapping it Up

A Revocable Living Trusts is one of the most powerful and flexible estate planning tools we have. They can to be used to accomplish the planning goals and satisfy the planning needs for most people, and should always be looked at as a planning option. Of course, there is no single planning tool that is suitable for every person and a trust isn't right for everyone. That being said, in my experience the trust plan option is the best option for most of the people we serve. Trusts provide the most efficient and effective way to control property while a person is alive and well and if they become incapacitated and when a person passes away. They also provide a way to direct the distribution of assets after death to the right people, the right way, and at the right time. We'll spend the next chapter going into a much more detailed discussion of distribution methods.

# Chapter 12

## Protecting your Loved Ones

L iving trusts are extremely useful for planning an estate and avoiding Probate. However, their usefulness isn't limited to just this purpose. One of the most powerful reasons for using a living trust for estate planning is in protecting your loved ones.

## Two Ways to Make Distributions

Distributions can be made to a beneficiary in one of two ways: an "outright distribution" or a "distribution in trust."

With an "outright distribution," the assets being distributed to the beneficiary are just given to the beneficiary. If it's a house, the house is deeded directly to the beneficiary, who then owns the house in his or her own name. If it's money, the beneficiary is generally given a check for the amount, and they then deposit the check into an account in their name or they open a new account in their name. If the beneficiary is married, then they will usually title the property jointly with their spouse.

A "distribution in trust" is just like it sounds. Rather than distributing the assets to the beneficiary directly, the assets are given to a trust share for the benefit of the beneficiary. The Trustee of the trust share (which can be either the beneficiary or an independent third party) manages the assets for the beneficiary, making distributions to or for the benefit of the beneficiary.

## The Problem with Making Outright Distributions

Outright distributions to a beneficiary leave the inherited assets vulnerable and subject to a variety of risks. The power of using Revocable Living Trusts in your estate planning comes from planning to avoid those risks for your beneficiaries. By making the distributions in trust, you are able to structure the inheritance for your beneficiaries in a way that is best for each individual.

## Different Approaches for Different Issues

There are three different situations where you would either need or want to design your estate plan in a way that provides protections for your beneficiaries. The first is where your beneficiary CAN'T manage the inherited assets on their own. The second is where the beneficiary SHOULD NOT manage the assets on their own. The third is where the beneficiary COULD manage well on their own, but you'd still like to protect from the "what ifs" of life. Let's look at each of these situations and look at ways to protect the inheritance for those beneficiaries.

# Beneficiaries who CAN'T Manage their own Finances

Some of our beneficiaries are not able to manage their own property and financial affairs. The two most common situations where this arises is with minor beneficiaries and with incapacitated beneficiaries.

## *Minor Beneficiaries*

If a person is under the age of majority (age 18 in Ohio), then they are not legally capable of owning property and managing it on their own. If a minor inherits property, then instead of the property being given directly to them, a Guardianship proceeding is established in the Probate Court for them in order to have someone else manage the property for them.

Rather than leave an inheritance outright to a minor beneficiary, it's much better to leave the assets to them in trust. With this approach, someone else can manage the assets for the child until they reach an age when you believe that they would be more capable of making responsible investing and spending decisions. While the law says that once the minor turns age 18 they can have full access to and control over their inherited funds, you may be more comfortable with an older age, like 25 or 30. While the assets are in trust with someone else serving as the Trustee, the Trustee will use the assets to provide for the beneficiary's needs (housing and living expenses, medical care, transportation, education, etc.).

If you have minor children, we explore this issue much more in depth in Chapter 15.

## *Incapacitated Beneficiaries*

As with minors, someone who has been declared incompetent isn't legally capable of managing their assets on their own. In these situations as well, a Guardianship is established for the beneficiary and a Guardian is appointed to manage the assets for the beneficiary.

Once again, the better approach for these beneficiaries is to leave their inheritance to them in trust. The Trustee of the trust share manages the assets for the beneficiary and distributes the assets in a way that is in the beneficiary's best interests.

## Beneficiaries who SHOULD NOT Manage their own Finances

While some beneficiaries are not legally capable and thus can't manage their own property and financial affairs, other beneficiaries are legally able to do so, but for some reason it would be inadvisable for them to do so. The most common issues we see in this category are (1) beneficiaries who don't have much experience managing finances, (2) beneficiaries who are "financially immature," (3) beneficiaries with addiction issues, and (4) beneficiaries with creditor issues.

## Financial Inexperience

Some beneficiaries simply do not have the experience of dealing with money. They've never had to make decisions about how to invest wisely, and have never had to decide the best way to save or spend a lump sum. This is especially true of younger people, generally those who are starting out in life, starting out in their jobs or careers, and are in the "building up phase" of their financial lives.

For these beneficiaries, some Trustmakers will choose to hold their distribution in trust for a period of time. They will instruct their Successor Trustee to manage the trust share for the beneficiary and make distributions to and for the beneficiary during the initial phase of the trust administration. The Successor Trustee will use his or her judgment and experience to make good decisions for the benefit of the beneficiary.

In some cases, the Trustmakers may have the beneficiary serve as a Co-Trustee of their trust share. This is a great way to teach the beneficiary how to make good decisions with the inherited assets: while they are serving as a Co-Trustee with the other Successor Trustee , they will be involved in the investing and spending decisions, will be involved in the distribution decisions, and will gain the needed experience. After a period of time, the beneficiary could become the sole Trustee, making them solely responsible for the trust assets, or the trust share could call for an outright distribution to the beneficiary after an initial period of time (a learning phase to gain financial experience).

## *Financial Immaturity*

Financial immaturity is a nicer way of stating that a beneficiary makes bad financial decisions. Unlike decisions born out of inexperience, a beneficiary who is financially immature will make their decisions based on poor financial judgment. In some cases, we refer to these types of beneficiaries as "spenders" or "spendthrifts."

One way of looking at it is how the people would respond if they received an unexpected windfall, like winning a lottery. Would they be the kind of person who would be wise in using the money, or would they go on a spending spree? Would they have money spent before they even received the check, or would they make good decisions?

We meet with clients all the time who have a child who is a spender. You may know someone like this, or you may have a child who falls into this category as well. You know the type, at any rate. A spender is someone who will spend $10 when they are given five dollars. As soon as they receive any money, it's already been spent.

In cases like these, the Trustmakers generally want to avoid giving the inheritance outright to the beneficiaries. Instead, they will instruct the Successor Trustee to administer the trust share for the beneficiary, having the Successor Trustee make the investing and spending decisions. The Successor Trustee, someone they choose who has good financial judgment and maturity, will decide how the beneficiary's assets should be invested and spent for the beneficiary.

## Addiction Issues

Unfortunately, we see too many people these days whose families have been impacted by addiction. For example, we see grandparents raising their grandchildren because of drug addiction. The opioid crisis has taken its toll on thousands of Ohio individual and families, either because a family member has overdosed and died or because they are incapable of taking care of themselves or anyone else anymore. In the context of estate planning, we are not only concerned about drug addition, but also alcohol and gambling addictions as well.

The issue is the danger involved in giving an addicted person a "no strings attached" outright distribution from an estate. It's not hard to imagine that within a few days, weeks or months the inheritance would be gone, used to support their addiction.

A few years ago I was contacted by a woman whose 43-year-old son had recently died. The son had received a lump sum settlement of about $160,000 from a personal injury claim and had spent $80,000 of it in two months. Sadly, he died from a drug overdose. As we administered his estate and looked at his accounts, we saw that he was withdrawing $3,000 and $4,000 in cash from his account every few days. It's not a stretch to say that the lump sum settlement contributed to his early death. And while a lump sum settlement of a personal injury claim isn't the same thing as an outright distribution from an estate, the results can be exactly the same. Unrestricted, no strings attached access to money can be devastating for some people.

The solution in cases like these isn't necessarily to disinherit those people. Instead, the assets could be left for the beneficiary in trust, with the Successor Trustee managing the funds as appropriate. The assets could even be used to get the beneficiary into an appropriate rehab program.

## *Creditor Issues*

Some of our clients want to protect their beneficiary's future inheritance by protecting it from the beneficiary's creditors. They are concerned that if an inheritance would be given outright to the beneficiary, the entire inheritance, or a substantial part of it anyway, would be taken by the beneficiary's creditors.

Just like in the case of addiction issues, the best solution for these beneficiaries is to have the assets held in a trust for the beneficiary. When the trust share assets are being managed by the Successor Trustee and the beneficiary doesn't have control over the assets, the beneficiary's creditors can't reach the assets and can't compel the beneficiary to withdraw trust share assets to satisfy their debt. If the Trustee is given discretion to make distributions to the beneficiary or not, as the Trustee determines to be in the beneficiary's best interest, the Successor Trustee can decide whether to make a distribution to the beneficiary to pay a debt or not.

# Beneficiaries who CAN Manage their own Finances

Most of our clients don't find themselves in the situation where they are dealing with any of the above issues. Probably 75% of our clients who have adult children who are mature and responsible and who could manage an inheritance very well. Our clients tell us that their kids are "doing just fine."

Still, most of our clients choose to add the enhanced protections of leaving an inheritance in trust for their beneficiaries. People understand that while things are OK now, things can change in an instant. There are unknowns out there that could pop up at any time that could put the inheritance or the beneficiary at risk. Here are the two issues we see most often:

## *Beneficiary gets Divorced*

One of the most common reasons why the Trustmaker may want to protect their beneficiary's inheritance is because of the possibility of a divorce. Let's face it, a high percentage of all marriages today end in divorce.

Some people are concerned that their beneficiary could lose half of their inheritance in a divorce proceeding. They want to make sure that the future ex-daughter-in-law or ex-son-in-law doesn't receive half of the inheritance.

Now you may be reading this and wondering what the concern is. An inheritance isn't marital property and isn't subject to being divided in a divorce proceeding, right? If you're thinking that, then you're correct. An inheritance isn't marital property, and isn't therefore subject to being divided in a divorce proceeding.

The problem arises when an inheritance is given outright to a beneficiary. In most cases, the beneficiary will receive the assets (usually in the form of a check), and will commingle the inherited assets with their marital assets. They will deposit the check into an account that is joined with their spouse. Once this is done and the money in the account is used to pay bills or any other use, it's impossible to tell which money in the account was the inheritance and which was the marital property.

By leaving the inheritance to the beneficiary in a trust, the beneficiary can't co-mingle the inherited assets with their marital assets. It will be kept separate and will be identifiable in the event of a divorce.

## *Beneficiary dies*

As we discussed in Chapter 11, when a trust is designed the Trustmaker chooses their primary beneficiaries, and they also choose contingent beneficiaries (the people who would receive the assets if the primary beneficiary isn't living at the time of distribution). In most cases, people will choose their children as their primary beneficiaries and their grandchildren as their contingent. The language usually looks something like this:

*"Upon the death of me and my spouse, my property shall be distributed to my children, in equal shares. If any of my children predeceases me, then that child's share shall be distributed in equal shares to that child's descendants."*

We refer to this as a "bloodline distribution" because the assets will go to someone who is a blood descendant of the decedent. Many people want their assets to go to their family and not to go to someone outside the family.

The risk with an outright distribution is that it leaves assets susceptible to going outside the family. Here's the scenario:

*John states in his Will that his assets should go to his daughter Anne, but if Anne isn't living, then the assets should go to her children in equal shares.*

*John dies and Anne is living, and all of John's assets pass outright to Anne. Six months later Anne dies. Anne's Will leaves everything to her husband Bill, and states that if Bill isn't living, then the assets go to her children in equal shares.*

*Bill is living when Anne dies so he receives all of her assets, including the assets that Anne had inherited from her father John. John wanted his assets to go to his grandchildren and not to his son-in-law, but because they were given to Anne in an outright distribution, John's wishes weren't carried out.*

Instead of leaving the assets in an outright distribution, if the assets were left in trust for the beneficiary the Trustmaker's wishes will be followed. Here's how that scenario plays out:

# Structuring A Trust Share For Protection

There are countless ways to structure a trust share to protect the beneficiary and the inheritance. The technique used will depend upon the needs of the beneficiary, the planning goals, and the Trustmaker's wishes.

# Beneficiaries who Can't or Should Not Manage Assets

Ultimately, the protection from using a trust share for a beneficiary who can't or should not manage their own assets comes from the fact that control of and access to the assets in the trust share are not given to the beneficiary. Someone else, namely the Successor Trustee, is given control over the assets and will make the decisions for the investing and spending of the trust share assets. The Successor Trustee will use the assets in the trust solely for the benefit of the beneficiary, but will use their judgment to determine how to best use the assets for the beneficiary.

For example, the Successor Trustee may be instructed to use the trust assets and make distributions to or for the beneficiary to pay for the beneficiary's health, education, or maintenance needs. This allows the Successor Trustee to use the assets in the trust share to pay for whatever needs a beneficiary may have. If they need money to pay for tuition, or books, or a car, or medical care, or groceries, or clothes, then the Trustee can distribute funds for those purposes. This instruction gives the

Successor Trustee broad discretion to use the trust assets in the beneficiary's best interests.

In situations where the beneficiary needs the protections of the trust share because they are too young or too inexperienced with handing money to receive the inheritance in an outright distribution, there can also be instructions to the Successor Trustee to distribute principal to the beneficiary at certain times or intervals. This can be done in lots of different ways. For example:

- The Trustee can be instructed to distribute all of the remaining principal in the trust share to the beneficiary when a certain event occurs, such as the beneficiary reaching a certain age;

- The Trustee could be instructed to distribute a portion of the remaining trust assets to the beneficiary when the beneficiary reaches a certain age, another percentage when the beneficiary reaches another age, and the remaining principal at another age (for example, 25% of age 25, another 25% at age 30, and the remainder at age 35); or

- The Successor Trustee could be instructed to distribute a portion of trust principal to the beneficiary after a certain amount of time has passed, and make subsequent distributions to the beneficiary at intervals (for example, 10% immediately on the formation of the trust share, another 25% three years later, another 25% three years after that, and the balance 5 years after that).

The idea with the staggered distributions of principal in the second two examples above is that the beneficiary isn't given all of the principal all at once, and they have an opportunity to "learn from their early mistakes." As subsequent distributions of principal are made, they are older and hopefully wiser.

## Protecting Beneficiaries Who Can Manage their Own Assets

As we saw earlier, most of our clients have beneficiaries who would be "just fine" managing an inheritance, but they still want to provide the protections of an inheritance in trust. In those cases, we recommend that we create "Convenience Shares" for the beneficiaries. These are trust shares for the beneficiary where the beneficiary also serves as the Trustee of the trust share. This allows the beneficiary to still be in control of the trust share assets and make all of the decisions about how the assets are invested and ultimately distributed to themselves, but also gives them the protections of the trust share against the possibility of a divorce, unforeseen creditors, or having the assets pass outside the family.

# Wrapping It Up

As you can see, using a trust to build in protections for beneficiaries is a very powerful way to design an estate plan. Every situation is different, with different assets, different beneficiaries with different strengths and different challenges, and every family will have different needs and goals. Taking all of these things into consideration, we are able to design a trust plan that will provide the necessary or desirable protections for every kind of beneficiary.

# Chapter 13

# Asset Alignment

In order for your estate plan to work correctly and meet the goals you designed it to meet, your assets must be properly aligned with the estate plan. It doesn't do much good to have a Will that directs your assets to a particular person but also have a beneficiary designation on your assets to someone else. If you have a Revocable Living Trust and you want your estate to avoid Probate, then the ownership of some of your assets needs to be changed in order to assure that those assets avoid Probate. *"Having a Trust"* doesn't make your estate avoid Probate. *"Having a Trust and having your assets properly aligned with the Trust"* makes your estate avoid Probate. Proper Asset Alignment is the single most important factor in determining the success of your estate plan.

Asset Alignment (sometimes called "funding") is the process of making changes to your assets – either ownership changes or beneficiary designation changes, or both – so that your assets work correctly with your estate plan. For the most part, Asset Alignment is usually done in connection with the creation of a trust plan, although other types of estate plans may also require some changes to assets. In this chapter, we'll focus on Asset Alignment with a trust plan.

# Aligning your Assets with your Trust

If you have a Revocable Living Trust, then it's safe to say that one of the purposes of the RLT is to avoid Probate for your estate. As I mentioned back in Chapter 9, "avoiding Probate" is pretty much a universally-held goal for people who enter into trusts for their estate plans. In order for your trust plan to have your estate avoid Probate, then the ownership of some of your assets will have to be changed.

If one of your goals for your estate plan is to provide your beneficiaries with some protections by making distributions to them in ongoing trust shares, then you'll need to make sure that any assets that by-pass probate by way of beneficiary designations will end up going through the trust as well.

## Changing Ownership of Certain Assets

For certain assets, asset alignment is done by changing ownership of the assets. The asset will be transferred to the trust. This means that the Trustee of the trust will be the new owner of the assets and will be the one to manage and use the asset.

At this point in the discussion, some clients will have a look of concern on their face. They don't want to give control of their assets to anyone else. It's at this point that I remind them that they will be the initial Trustees of their trust, so they are the one who will have control over the asset. By giving the asset to their trust, they are really giving the asset to themselves as Trustee of the trust. They will still have complete control over their assets and they don't have to go to anyone for permission to do anything they want with the assets. As the Trustmaker, the initial Trustee and the initial beneficiary of the trust, they don't give up anything by retitling assets into the trust.

The purpose of re-titling assets into the RLT is to give the Trustee of the trust access to and control over the assets. Why do we have to do it this way? To answer this question, we need to re-examine why assets go through Probate.

Do you remember the reason why estates have to go through Probate in the first place? Back in Chapter 7 I said that the purpose of a Probate estate administration proceeding is to provide a legal process for the handling of the deceased person's assets. This is necessary for assets that are owned by a person when they die if there is no joint owner and no beneficiary designation directing the distribution of the asset. In these situations, Probate involvement is needed so that the Probate Court can give a person (the Executor or the Administrator) the legal authority to access and/or sell the deceased person's assets.

If a person dies when their assets are owned in a trust, then those assets don't have to go through Probate in order for the right person to access and/or sell those assets. Probate Court involvement isn't needed to give a person the legal authority. This is because the trust is the legal owner of the assets, and the trust has Successor Trustees who are named in the trust and who are already legally empowered to access and manage the trust's assets. The Successor Trustee doesn't need anything from the Probate Court in order to do his or her job as Successor Trustee.

# Which Assets need to be Owned by the Trust?

The basic rule of Asset Alignment is any asset is transferred to the RLT if that asset would have to go through Probate if the owner dies while owning that asset. If the asset already by-passes Probate with a beneficiary designation, then trust ownership isn't necessary for Probate avoidance but is still sometimes a good idea.

The most common assets that need to be transferred into the trust are the following:

- **Bank accounts.** This includes checking and savings accounts, money market accounts, and Certificates of Deposit. The banks are requested to re-title the accounts into the name of the trust, and the Trustees sign new signature cards as Trustees so they have access. It's not necessary for the bank to close the existing accounts and open new accounts. They keep the same accounts open and show that the trust is the new owner with the Trustees having access.

- **Real estate.** This includes residential and commercial properties, personal homes and rental properties held as investment. Note, however, that if any properties are owned in a business entity like an LLC or a corporation, then the real estate owned by the entity doesn't need to be re-titled. Instead, when the business is transferred into the trust (see below) the assets of the business - including the real estate – go into the trust as a part of the business.

- **Investment accounts.** This includes mutual funds and stock and bond portfolio accounts. HOWEVER, this doesn't include any retirement accounts. Retirement

Accounts are handled differently and are discussed in the section below on Changing Beneficiary Designations.

- **Motor vehicles.** Any vehicle that has a title showing ownership must be transferred into the trust. This includes cars, trucks, boats, and recreational vehicles. A new title is issued at the Auto Title Office showing ownership in the trust. However, if there is still a lien on the vehicles, the title can't be changed until after the lien has been cancelled.

- **Stocks and Bonds.** If a person owns individual shares of stock, whether in certificate form or in a "street account" (like a Computershare account), then the stock needs to be re-titled to the trust. Also, any US Savings Bonds will need to be re-issued to the trust.

- **Business interests.** If you own an interest in a closely-held business (usually in the form of an LLC or a corporation), then those business interests will need to be transferred to the trust. If you are the sole owner, we typically do the transfer through an Assignment of Interest document. If there are other Co-Owners of the business, then the entity agreements (LLC Operating Agreement or Corporate By-Laws) will determine whether and how your ownership interest can be transferred. Your estate planning attorney will need to examine those entity agreements and advise you on the alignment of your business interest with your trust plan

## Changing Beneficiaries on Certain Assets

We saw in the previous section that certain assets should have their ownership changed to the trust. However, ownership should not be changed for all types of assets. In some cases, if the ownership is changed to the trust there will be significant penalties for making the transfer. In other cases, changing the ownership isn't needed in order to accomplish the planning goals. For those assets, we instead change the beneficiary of the assets to coordinate with the trust planning goals.

## Retirement Accounts

For retirement accounts, it's very important to remember that the ownership of the retirement account should NOT be changed. Take a traditional IRA, for example. You know that if you withdraw money out of your traditional IRA, that withdrawn amount is all taxable income and you will have to pay tax on the amount you withdrew. If you have not yet reached the age of 59 1/2, you would also have to pay a 10% penalty on the amount withdrawn.

If you change the ownership of your IRA to your trust (even to yourself as Trustee of the trust), the IRS would treat that transfer as the withdrawal of the entire IRA. You would owe tax on the entire amount. *This is obviously not a good result, and should be avoided at all costs.*

Instead of changing the ownership of the IRA, the IRA should remain in your name. Depending on the design of the trust plan you may want to change the beneficiaries on the IRA. Let's look at a couple of examples:

## Scenario 1

## An Outright Distribution Plan

*John is married to Jane and they have three children. John's trust plan leaves all of his assets to Jane upon his* death and states that if Jane isn't living, the assets are to be distributed outright to their children. John has a traditional IRA.

John should make sure that Jane is the primary beneficiary of his IRA, and that his three children are the contingent beneficiaries. In this case, there is no need to make the trust a beneficiary of the IRA since all assets are being distributed to John's children outright and free of the trust.

## Scenario 2

## Planning for Ongoing Protections

John is married to Jane and they have three children. John's trust plan leaves all of his assets to Jane upon his death and states that if Jane isn't living, the assets are to be distributed in trust shares for the benefit of their children. John has a traditional IRA.

John should make sure that Jane is the primary beneficiary of his IRA and should make the trust the contingent beneficiary.

If Jane survives John, then she can assume the IRA, making it her own. If Jane does not survive John, then the IRA will be transferred to the trust at John's death. The IRA will then be split among the trust shares for the three children and managed by the Trustee as inherited IRAs. This arrangement allows the IRA to have the protections of the trust share along with the other assets of the trust.

The changes to be made to retirement accounts can have a very immediate and significant legal and tax implications if done incorrectly, so it's critical that you consult with an experienced estate planning attorney before making any changes to your retirement accounts.

## *Life Insurance*

For life insurance policies, we recommend to our clients that they don't change the ownership of the insurance, but instead change the beneficiaries to reflect and accomplish their planning goals. Since life insurance has a beneficiary on it, the life insurance won't be subject to Probate (as long as the estate isn't the beneficiary). It's not necessary to change the ownership of the life insurance to the trust in order for it to avoid Probate.

That being said, it's usually best to change the trust the beneficiary of the life insurance. When the owner/insured dies, the life insurance company will pay the death benefit to the Trustee of the trust. The Trustee will then use the death benefit to pay the estate's expenses and taxes and, if there is any left over, will then use the assets as instructed in the trust (either making outright distributions to the beneficiaries or holding the remainder in trust and making distributions for the beneficiaries as the trust directs).

## Wrapping it Up

Proper Asset Alignment is the single most important factor in determining the success of your estate plan. Simply having a Trust doesn't do it. Your assets must be properly aligned with the plan in order for your goals to be accomplished. And as we'll see in the next chapter, Asset Alignment isn't something that only needs to be done once. It's something that needs to be kept up at all times as assets are bought and sold and accounts are opened and closed. I can't overemphasize the importance of having your assets properly aligned with your trust plan.

# Chapter 14

# *Maintaining Your Plan*

S ome people believe that once their estate plan has been completed, they never need to think about it or look at it again. They believe that it will be effective when it's needed, no matter what happens. They view their estate planning as a singular event, something they do once and never have to think about again. However, one of the only constant things in our lives is change.

A client typically comes into the estate planning appointment saying things like "I want a will" or "I need to name guardians for my children." They say things like "I want to protect my assets." However, these statements are all "whats." As I've shown in this book, the "what" isn't as important as the "why" the planning is being done.

The reason people do estate planning isn't to get a stack of legal documents. They get an estate plan to achieve a certain result from those legal documents. They want to:

- "avoid Probate so my family will have an easier time when I pass away than I did when my parents died" or

- "make sure my kids receive their inheritance at a specific age and give someone else control until then" or

- "make sure as much of my money as possible goes to my family."

What it all boils down to is you want an estate plan so that your loved ones will be taken care of at the appropriate time. You want your estate plan to work when it's needed. It's up to the estate planning attorney to help you get past the "what you want" and find out "why you want it." It's critical that your goals be properly identified so your plan can achieve everything it needs to achieve. And once your goals are identified and the legal documents are in place to achieve those goals, the process has not come to an end. In fact, it's just begun.

Let me share with you a little-known secret about estate planning that I've discovered over the years I've been working as an estate planning attorney: *the ultimate success of your estate plan isn't about the documents.* It's NOT about whether you have a Will-based plan or a Trust-based plan. *The single biggest determining factor of whether an estate plan is successful is whether it achieves your goals at the time it's needed* (when you die or if you become incapacitated). Which means that in order for your plan to work, all of the following need to happen:

- your goals need to be identified,
- you must choose the right kind of plan (Will or Trust) to achieve those goals;
- your plan documents must be written in a way to achieve those goals,
- your assets must be aligned with your goals and plan documents, and
- everything must be kept up to date as things change through the years.

Your estate plan needs to work at some unspecified time in the future. At the time that it's needed, there may be new laws in effect, new assets owned, different circumstances in your life, your children's lives, and in the lives of the people you choose to serve as your Successor Trustees, Agents, Guardians and Executors., You may have different needs and goals for your estate plan. So the question is: "*Why would you ever do an estate plan with all of these variables and NOT keep the plan up to date?*"

You already know how important it is to maintain things.

You maintain your car by giving it regular oil changes, keeping the tires well-inflated and buying new tires when needed. You not only get things fixed when they are broken, but you also do preventative maintenance to keep small issues from becoming bigger and much more expensive.

You go to the doctor on a regular basis to have check-ups, even when you're feeling just fine. Again, you take preventative steps to identify things and head them off before they become major issues.

Estate plan maintenance is the same idea: things change over time, and your estate plan needs to be maintained to keep it working properly. As things change in your life, your estate plan must be updated and maintained to keep up with the changes.

## Ways to Maintain an Estate Plan

There are basically two ways to maintain an estate plan. The first is to get things updated when you identify things that need to be changed. That might be a change in the percentages that you are leaving to your beneficiaries, for example, or it could be changing the people who will be in charge of certain aspects of the estate plan. The second way is to engage in a regular, formalized program where (1) your plan details are is reviewed on a regular basis to see if changes are needed and (2) your asset alignment is reviewed to make sure that asset ownership and beneficiary designations are still up-to-date.

## Maintenance "as Needed"

Going to see your estate planning attorney only when you've identified something that you want to change may seem like the most efficient approach. After all, there's no need to incur the expense unless something needs to be changed, right?

The problem with the "as needed" maintenance approach is that it often doesn't work. We've seen over the years that clients do their estate plans, put them on the shelf, and don't give them another thought. Years and years go by, and the plan is "out of sight, out of mind." So changes that should be made aren't ever made.

We've had families come to us with estate plans that their parents had done 20 and 25 years earlier, with no maintenance or changes to the plans over the intervening years. The plans were completely out-of-date and failed to keep up with the families' needs.

We've had clients with trust plans come back to us 4 or 5 years after completing their trust plans, and although all of their assets had been property aligned with the estate plan, they no longer owned half of the originally-owned assets and had new assets that weren't properly aligned with their planning.

## Formal Updating Programs

The more effective way to maintain an estate plan is to engage in a regular formal program. In our office we have a Continuing Care Program that we offer to our clients. Our Continuing Care Program is an annual membership program that clients have the option to participate in every year. The purpose of our Continuing Care Program is to make it as easy as possible for our clients to keep their trust plans working at their best so it can take care of them and their beneficiaries and accomplish the rest of their planning goals. For the clients who participate in our Continuing Care Program, we help them make sure that the plan will work correctly for them when it's needed.

Every year we do an estate plan design review for our Continuing Care Program clients. We look at their plan design and explore whether they need or want to make any changes to the "who," the "what" or the "how" in the plan documents. We remind them of the different options they have and how things might work differently or better under changed circumstances. And when changes are needed, those changes are made at no additional cost to the clients. It's all included in the annual fee.

In addition to the plan design changes, we do an Asset Alignment review. As we saw in Chapter 13, the importance of proper Asset Alignment can't be overstated, so it's critical that assets be reviewed to make sure everything stays aligned. We see that people are always buying and selling things like real estate and cars, and we often see that those newly acquired assets aren't titled in the trust. The same is true for bank accounts and investment accounts. We see that some clients have taken their 401(k) or 403(b) and have rolled it into an IRA but didn't keep the beneficiary designations aligned with the trust goals. As a part of our Continuing Care Program we help our clients get those newly acquired assets correctly aligned with the estate plan.

## Wrapping it Up

We all want to have a perfectly prepared estate plan with perfectly aligned assets. But the fact of the matter is that no matter how well your estate plan was designed and drafted, and no matter how well your assets were originally aligned with your estate plan, the plan will need to be kept up to date. Your estate plan will need to be maintained as the laws change, as your family changes, as your assets change, and as your needs and goals change.

# Chapter 15

# Estate Planning for Families with Young Children

A s we've seen throughout this book, every family will have its own particular needs when it comes to how they should do their estate planning. They need to look at their personal situation, their beneficiaries' strengths and challenges, the amount and type of assets they own, and the goals they'd like to achieve. The plan they end up with will be one that lines up with all of their circumstances and achieves all of their goals. There is no "one size fits all."

Having said that, if you have children under the age of 18, you have some very specific estate planning needs that you need to address in your estate plan. You are probably already aware of some, like the need to name a guardian for your children so the right person will be in charge of taking care of your children if something happens to you before they turn 18. Other issues may be unfamiliar to you, although we've touched briefly on them. We'll explore the issues here in this chapter.

Probably the easiest way to look at the issues is to examine the most common mistakes I see parents of young children making in their estate plans. My role is to help these parents see the issues and avoid those mistakes in their estate plans, and my hope is to help you understand and avoid those mistakes as well. The biggest mistakes we see are:

- Naming your children as Beneficiaries
- Thinking you don't have an "Estate"
- Getting stuck on who to name as Guardian
- Naming Guardians as Beneficiaries
- Procrastinating

Let's examine the 5 biggest mistakes so you can make sure your plan doesn't have them, or so that you can fix your plan if it does.

# Mistake #1:
# Naming Your Minor Children as Beneficiaries in Your Planning

No, you didn't read that wrong.

The **biggest** and **most common** mistake that parents make in their estate planning is naming their children as beneficiaries. That includes:

- Beneficiaries in their Wills;
- Beneficiaries of their retirement accounts; and
- Beneficiaries of their life insurance.

Don't worry, I'm not suggesting that parents should disinherit their children. We have a responsibility to provide for our children, and to the extent that we are able, we need to provide for them in our estate plans. If the unexpected happens, then we need to have the plans in place to make sure that our children will be taken care of. However, naming your minor children directly as the beneficiaries is the <u>absolute wrong way</u> to do it.

## "What's The Problem with Naming our Kids as Beneficiaries?"

The problem with naming our young children as beneficiaries is that while they are minors, they are not capable of owning property, and when they turn 18 and become adults they're generally not ready to make sound, responsible decisions with money.

When a minor inherits property (whether it's through a Will, a life insurance policy, or a retirement plan), a **Guardianship of the Estate** must be established through the Probate Court for the management of that property. Minors can't own property, so a Guardian must be appointed to manage the property for them. We looked very briefly at guardianships in Chapter 7 but didn't go too deep at the time. However, guardianships are at the very heart of the matter when it comes to planning for minor children and we need to look a lot more closely at how they work.

## "So What's the Problem with a Guardianship of the Estate?"

There are a lot of problems with a Guardianship of the Estate, but the biggest is the fact that the Guardianship ends when the child turns 18.

As stated previously, when a child turns 18 she is an adult and under the law can own and manage her own property, so there is no longer a need to have a Guardian manage her assets for her. The Guardianship is therefore terminated, and the Guardian distributes all of the assets remaining in the Guardianship estate to the child. At this point, the child can manage her own assets and spend it as she sees fit. Since she is an adult, she can do whatever she wants with her assets without any guidance or supervision. This is true whether she is being given $5,000 or $500,000.

Be honest with yourself. Would you give an 18-year-old $500,000 – with no strings attached? How about $100,000? Maybe $50,000? Would you feel comfortable giving any significant amount of money to your children when they turn 18? That's exactly what happens when a Guardianship of the Estate is terminated.

## *"What's the Solution?"*

If the problem with naming your children as your beneficiaries is that a Guardianship of the Estate would be necessary, then you need to have a plan that avoids the Guardianship of the Estate without disinheriting your children. The solution is creating a Revocable Living Trust.

With a Trust, the property doesn't go directly to the children, so a Guardianship of the Estate isn't required. Instead, the property is held in a trust share for your child and is used by your Successor Trustee to take care of your child's needs. If you pass away while your children are still too young to make good financial decisions and are still too financially inexperienced to be on their own with an inheritance, the Trust will be there to protect them.

With a Trust, you can establish the rules for how and when distributions are made to or for your children. While they are still young, the assets can be used to provide for their needs. The person who is in charge of their well-being (the "Guardian of the Person" – more on that later) can be given money from the Trust to provide for their education, their healthcare, and their general living expenses. And, unlike a Guardianship of the Estate, the Trust doesn't have to require a full distribution of all of the assets when the child turns 18.

In fact, that's one of the most powerful aspects of Trust Planning for younger children: the ability to require the Trustee of the Trust to continue to hold the assets in the Trust (still making distributions for the needs of the child) until the child is old enough and mature enough to make good financial decisions on his or her own.

Consider these 2 very different examples:

## *Example #1*

*John and Mary have one son, Jack. When Jack is only 5 years old, John and Mary are in a fatal car accident. John and Mary weren't "wealthy," but together they had $1 million in life insurance.*

*John and Mary had planned their estates with Wills, and had named Jack as their contingent beneficiary on their life insurance. A Guardian of the Estate is appointed by the Probate Court to manage the assets for Jack, under the court's supervision. The Guardian pays for Jack's needs as approved in advance by the Probate Court. When Jack turns 18, the remaining assets ($850,000) are turned over to Jack.*

*Jack, who is about to graduate from high school, becomes the life of the party with his new-found riches. He buys a new sports car and starts to spend his money on all of the things he and his friends want. He decides that college really isn't something he needs to do, and tries his hand at some day trading in the stock market.*

*Two years later, with almost all of money gone and nothing to show for it, Jack realizes – too late - that he should have made some very different decisions with his life and his money.*

## Example #2

*John and Mary have one son, Jack. When Jack is only 5 years old, John and Mary are in a fatal car accident. John and Mary weren't "wealthy," but together they had $1 million in life insurance.*

*John and Mary had created their estate plan using a Revocable Living Trust, and they named their Trust as the beneficiary of their life insurance. In this case, a Guardianship of the Estate doesn't have to be set up, since Jack isn't the direct beneficiary of any of the assets (although he is the sole beneficiary of the Trust). The Trustee of the Trust uses the assets of the trust to pay for all of Jack's needs. When Jack turns 18, the Trustee uses some of the trust assets to throw Jack a high school graduation party and to buy Jack a good, dependable (and sensible) car.*

*The next fall, Jack enrolls in college, with the Trustee paying the tuition and expenses from the Trust assets. The Trustee continues to pay Jack's living expenses and medical expenses as well.*

*Seven years later, Jack is 25. He has a bachelor's degree and a master's degree in hand and a bright future in front of him. He's now working at a good job, has started saving money for his own retirement, and is thinking about getting married. At that point, the*

*Trustee distributes the money remaining in the trust ($800,000) to Jack.*

Which of these 2 examples sounds more appealing to you? The answer is obvious, of course. Example #2, using the Revocable Living Trust, has Jack in a much better situation in his life.

Right now you're probably wondering whether a Revocable Living Trust estate plan is something you should consider, but you may be thinking you don't really have an "estate" to worry about. That leads us right into Mistake #2.

# Mistake #2
# Thinking You Don't Have
# "an Estate" to Plan

We often hear from younger parents that they don't need to do "estate planning" because they don't have an "estate." They feel that because they don't have a lot saved up yet, have little equity in their home, and are just getting started with their retirement plans, they have nothing to plan for. In their minds, an "estate" is something that wealthy people have, and they certainly wouldn't include themselves in that category – at least not yet.

However, while many parents of younger children don't have a lot on their current balance sheets, they do have something to protect their families if they should pass away prematurely – life insurance. Parents will often purchase life insurance on the life of one or both parents, depending on their circumstances, needs, and goals, in case the unexpected happens. They want to make sure that their family has enough money to survive the loss of one or both incomes, as well as provide for the children if both parents are gone. They may want to make sure there is sufficient money available to pay the mortgage on their home and/or fund college educations and weddings. If both parents pass away, it's often this life insurance that provides the majority of an inheritance for the minor children.

Think back to the "Estate Calculator Worksheet" at the end of chapter 1. It's helpful to go through the exercise of calculating the size of your estate to see just what your beneficiaries may inherit. If you didn't go through that exercise, we've got an abbreviated version here that helps you see the *per person* inheritance as it now stands.

1. Write the total approximate gross value of your assets (including your home, bank and investment accounts, and retirement accounts)

$_____

2. Write the total amount of your life insurance

$_____

3. Add lines 1 and 2 (this is your total gross estate)

$_____

4. Write the total of your debt (mortgage, credit cards, car loans, student loans, etc.)

$_____

5. Subtract line 4 from line 3 (this is your total net estate)

$_____

6. How many children do you have?

_____

7. Divide line 5 by line 6 (this is the    $_____
   total estate per child)

Are you comfortable with the possibility that if you passed away, your children could receive this amount (approximately) when they turn 18, **knowing they can do ANYTHING they want with the money?**

If you answer "No," then you need a Revocable Living Trust estate plan. This type of plan will allow you to protect your children and the assets they will receive.

# Mistake #3
# Getting Stuck on Who to
# Name as Guardian

As we saw in Chapter 7, there are 2 different kinds of Guardians: a Guardian of the Estate (the kind you want to avoid) and a Guardian of the Person.

The Guardian of the Person is appointed by the Probate Court just like the Guardian of the Estate, but the Guardian of the Person has nothing to do with the management and spending of money. Instead, the Guardian of the Person is that person who becomes legally responsible for your children, making sure they receive the care they need. This Guardian is responsible for seeing to it that your child is safe and secure, and is being cared for emotionally and physically. They can't replace you, but they can step in and provide for your children.

So many times, when I speak with younger parents about their estate planning they get stuck on the question of who to name as Guardian of the Person. They're trying to find the "perfect" Guardian. Unfortunately, there are so many different competing factors to consider, and sometimes people give up because they can't find the perfect person for the job.

I've found that approaching the problem methodically helps my clients find the right answer. I've developed a 4-step process to help my clients make the right decision for their particular situation.

## Four Steps to Choosing a Guardian of the Person

When deciding who you should name as the Guardian of the Person for your children, you should go through a process involving:

1. identifying potential candidates
2. listing factors or characteristics that are important to you
3. matching your candidates to those characteristics
4. discussing the matter with your top candidates

Let's look at each step in detail.

## Step One: Identify Potential Candidates

You'll need to make a list of everyone you know who might *possibly* be a good guardian for your children. It's not important (at this point) whether you think that they would agree to serve, or whether the circumstances would be ideal. When considering whether someone should be on the list, ask yourself, "*Would they provide a better home for my children than foster care?*" If the answer is yes, you should put them on your list.

## Step Two: Identify Important Factors and Characteristics

Now that you have a list of people as potential candidates, you need a way of identifying which of them would be the best choices for you and your family. You need to think about the factors that are most important to you in someone who could potentially be taking care of your children. Factors to consider when choosing a person to serve as Guardian of the Person may include, among other things, the prospect's:

- familial relationship to you;
- religious or spiritual beliefs;
- marital status;
- parenting style;
- stability (such as employment or residence);
- own children;
- age and maturity; and/or
- location

## Step Three: Match the People to your Priorities

The next step is to use the factors you chose in Step Two to narrow down your list of candidates from Step One. Obviously, the perfect choice for Guardian would score highly on every measure that is important to you. However, it's unlikely that any one person could match up exactly on every issue as the perfect choice, so you will likely have more success in choosing the factors that are most important to you. After going through your list of people and comparing them to your list of priorities, you'll end up with a short list of people who "made the cut."

## *Step Four: Talk with the Prospective Guardians*

You now need to speak with the people you're considering nominating as Guardians. If you aren't sure about someone's parenting style, for example, and that ranked high as an important factor to you, speak with your prospects and find out their philosophy for rearing children.

In addition to finding out more about your potential Guardians, it's always a good idea to let them know that you're considering them, and to get their agreement to serve if the need ever arises. Let them know why you've chosen them and what's important to you. Give the person time to think about the responsibility and consequences of becoming the Guardian of your children.

No one can replace you as your child's parent, and naming a Guardian isn't about finding the person who can do that. Naming the Guardian of the Person is about finding the best person possible, taking all of the factors into consideration. Instead of failing to get a plan in place because you can't think of the *perfect* person, go through the 4-step process above and find out who the *best* person would be.

# Mistake #4
# Naming Guardians as Beneficiaries

Some parents already understand that naming their children as beneficiaries (Mistake #1) is a bad idea. To avoid doing that, some parents have named the Guardian of the Person as the beneficiary of their life insurance and retirement accounts. In some cases, they were advised to do this by a well-meaning insurance agent or financial advisor. The idea behind this approach is that the Guardian (not the children) will receive the proceeds and a Guardianship of the Estate won't be necessary. They will hold onto the assets for the children and use them as needed.

However, there are several *major* problems with this technique.

First, when assets are paid to persons they *legally belong to* that person. They are entitled to do *anything they want* with the assets. They can use them for their own benefit, or for the benefit of their children as well as yours. They have no legally enforceable duty to protect the assets and use them solely for the benefit of your children.

Some people tell me that the person they're naming as Guardian would have a moral obligation to do the right thing, and that they trust that the Guardian would uphold that obligation. After all, the parents are trusting them with the care of their children, so wouldn't they trust them to handle the money correctly?

That may be the case. So let's assume that the Guardian would do the right thing and use the assets properly. That brings us to the next major problem, though. Even if the Guardian considers the assets as belonging to the children, the rest of the world won't, including any creditors or potential creditors of the Guardian.

If the Guardian runs into a problem with creditors, then any assets they have are subject to being attached to satisfy any judgment that could be entered against them. That would include the assets being held in the Guardian's name for the benefit of your children. Their creditors don't care that the money is meant for the care of your children. They only want to be paid from any source available to them, and an account with a pile of life insurance money is tops on their list.

Even if the Guardian doesn't have creditor issues, if the Guardian passes away with your kids' assets in their name, then those assets would be controlled by the Guardian's estate planning, not yours. It would likely pass to the Guardian's spouse or kids, instead of to your kids. Even if the Guardian did plan ahead and make sure those assets would go to your kids, they would then end up in a Guardianship of the Estate – exactly where we didn't want to be in the first place.

# Mistake #5
# Procrastinating

The final mistake parents make in their estate planning is putting it off. Whether their procrastination is due to being so busy with everyday living, with parenting, work, and finding a few minutes of down time, or is due to a reluctance to face these issues, the end result is the same: this essential planning doesn't get done.

Let's face the facts:

- We'll all eventually pass away;
- No one is guaranteed tomorrow (we never know when our time is up);
- There is a possibility that you could pass away before your children are adults; and
- If the right planning isn't done, you could leave your children in a real mess.

Admittedly, those aren't fun facts. The idea that you could die while your children are young is depressing. However, as difficult as it may be, and as busy are you are, your responsibility as a parent is to take the steps needed to get your planning in place. Our clients tell us that the **peace of mind** that comes from doing the right planning, from setting up a plan to protect and provide for your children, far outweighs anything else and makes it all worthwhile.

## Wrapping it Up

When you have minor children you need to address the special issues of this situation in your estate planning. Making sure that your children will be taken care of and making sure that whatever they inherit from you will be used appropriately to provide for them and their needs is of paramount importance. Making sure that any inherited assets will only be given to them when they are mature enough to make sound financial decisions is critical as well.

For a majority of parents who are aware of these issues, a Revocable Living Trust is the best solution. A Trust allows the assets to be held for your children and managed by someone you trust, and this person will use their judgment and discretion to distribute the assets for the benefit of your children. When your children are older and better able to manage things on their own, then then assets can be given to them to control.

# Conclusion

I t's my sincere hope that this book has been helpful to you and that you now have a much better idea of the issues and opportunities you have before you as you think about making or updating your estate plan.

However, all of the information in the world won't do you any good unless you act on it. Knowing what you need to do isn't the same as doing it. So take action now.

If you are anywhere in the State of Ohio we are able to assist you with your estate planning. We offer no cost initial consultations, either in our office or by video conference. In those consultations we review your current personal and financial situation, help you identify your planning goals, and review your current estate plan (if you have one) to see if it will meet your needs. If you want or need to make changes we help you design the plan that best meets all of your goals. You can either call my office at 419-872-7670 or request an appointment through my website: www.chamberlain-law.net.

If you're not in the State of Ohio, then I recommend that you meet with an experienced estate planning attorney who is licensed in your State. I'm a member of a national organization of estate planning attorneys and if you need help finding an experienced estate planning attorney in your area, I would be happy to help you find someone.

The best of luck to you in your planning!

WA